Strategy is to business as air is to life—essential, yet unseen. Properly channeled, air becomes wind and strategy becomes intelligent action—both unleashing unparalleled power visible to all.

SCULPTING
AIR

THE EXECUTIVE'S GUIDE
TO SHAPING STRATEGY

Rich Horwath

Published by:
Sculptura Consulting, Inc.
Barrington Hills, IL 60010

Printed in the United States of America

Publisher's – Cataloging-in-Publication Data

Horwath, Rich
    Sculpting Air: The Executive's Guide to Shaping Strategy/Rich Horwath.
    p. cm.
    Includes bibliographical references.
    ISBN 0-9747114-1-1
    1. Strategic planning. 2. Creative ability in business. 3. Business planning.
    I. Title
    HD30.28.H67   2005
    658.4'012—dc22

                                                            2005906750

www.sculpturaconsulting.com

For Anne, Luke and Jessica

&

Mom, Pop, Sharon, Dan and Gram

Contents

Acknowledgments

Shakespeare's comment, "There is nothing either good or bad, but thinking makes it so," is a premise on which I've conducted my research and tried to add to the body of strategy knowledge. In that journey, there are many people that have contributed to my learning, beginning with my mother and father, both of whom inspired and nurtured in me a passion for reading and writing. I am eternally grateful for the immeasurable time, energy, and love they invested in my development.

Special thanks go to Reggie Blackburn, Rick Davis, Andrew de Guttadauro, Dean Gregory, David Kushner, Dan Linden, and Rob Schneider—business leaders that graciously shared their business acumen and experiences with me to review and hone the content of the book. I am extremely grateful for their feedback, insights, and candor—all of which positively shaped the final outcome of the book.

I am very appreciative of the clients that have allowed me to contribute to their efforts through consulting projects and training programs. The hands-on strategy experience we've shared together has been invaluable and generated numerous insights for which I am extremely thankful. Special thanks to Laura Hamill, Chris Thompson, Susan Sybert, Dean Gregory, Rob Schneider, Ranndy Kellogg, David Kushner, Kelly Peacy, Phil Tegeler, Cinda Orr, Lisa Hempy, Dan Linden, Ron Bruns, Andrew de Guttadauro and Jeff Hackman.

Thanks to Jim Weems for creatively capturing the concept of the book with his cover design.

Thanks to Dawn Josephson and her team at Cameo Publications for devoting their copyediting talents to the book.

Thanks to Kevin Shuster for developing the illustrations used throughout the book.

Thanks to the strategy authors who have contributed to my learning and development through their work. I appreciate their research, insights and leadership in the field.

Finally, I'd like to thank all of my family and friends for their enduring support, kind words and thought-provoking discussions. I am blessed to have you all in my life.

CHAPTER 1

Sculpting Air

*Strategy is to business as air is to life—essential,
yet unseen. Properly channeled, air becomes wind
and strategy becomes intelligent action—both
unleashing unparalleled power visible to all.*

We can't see it. We can't touch it. Yet, our business can't thrive without it. Strategy—an abstract concept whose real-world presence influences how each and every one of us spends our time, money, and talent. With so much riding on strategy development's outcome, shouldn't we invest the time to do it well?

Strategy development can be likened to sculpting, both of which require the vision to foresee the finished form and the skill, insight, and craftsmanship to create it. We use the words "sculpting air" to capture the challenge of creating something that we cannot see—strategy. This book has been designed to provide you with a proven process and the tools to shape your business strategy. Whether you're developing strategy for a product, business unit, or a multi-billion dollar company, you will find a clear and concise roadmap on how to do it effectively and efficiently. That said, there are still a fair number of managers asking the question: "Does strategy matter?"

Foolish question, you say. Of course it does. Really? Then how do we explain the thousands of companies, products, and services that operate without a clear strategy in written form each year? The answer to the question "Does strategy matter?" can be either "yes" or "no," depending on the type of company. The answer will be "yes, strategy does matter" if a company is seeking long-term financial success.

However, the answer will be "no, strategy does not matter" if the company is married to a fire-drill mentality, thrives on daily crises, reacts and overreacts to every competitor move, changes direction based on one sales rep story from a tradeshow in Atlanta, and rationalizes that "we've done just fine without strategy." As Andrew Campbell, a former instructor at the Harvard Business School and the London Business School has said, "Almost every company I know needs a corporate strategy and doesn't have one."

Strategy: Fuel for Success

Research has proven the importance of strategy in business. The Evergreen Project is the most statistically rigorous management research ever conducted on the keys to enduring business success.[1] The study examined more than 200 management practices, from innovation and process reengineering to 360-degree performance reviews. A total of 160 companies were reviewed over a ten-year period to determine which management practices were essential to a company's financial success. The financial measurements used included the total return to shareholders, sales, assets, operating income, and return on invested capital.

The results showed that financially successful companies all had a clearly defined and well-articulated strategy. No exceptions. These companies outperformed the losing companies by a 945% to 62% margin in total return to shareholders, had a 415% to 83% advantage in sales, a 358% to 97% advantage in assets, a 326% to 22% advantage in operating income and a 5.45% to -8.52% advantage in return on invested capital.

While many companies have been able to survive without a clearly defined strategy in written form, a question looms: "How much better could they do if they had a strategy?" The 12% gain last year might seem impressive, unless it could have been a 65% gain with a solid strategy behind it. A company, product, or service can survive for a time without strategy, but it will never thrive. When CEO Edward Breen took over at scandal-ridden Tyco, one of the first things he did to right the ship was create a strategy development process. "The company never had a strategy-setting process. We now review that with our board," said Mr. Breen.[2]

Making Time for Strategy

If research has proven that strategy is critical to an organization's financial success, then surely we are all spending significant time developing, discussing, and reviewing it, right? Wrong. A study by the Economist Intelligence Unit examined how senior management team members (CEO, COO, CFO, business unit presidents, managing directors, etc.) from more than 180 companies worldwide spent their time together during the year.[3] Of the roughly 250 hours senior management teams invested in meeting together, only 15% of their time was spent on strategy issues. In fact, the research showed that senior management spent 80% of their time reviewing issues that represented less than 20% of their company's long-term value.

In the business planning workshops I conduct with organizations, many groups agree that the average time they spend on strategy development and review is less than 10% per month. If we know strategy is essential to our success, why aren't we spending more time on it?

Several reasons exist as to why we do not spend sufficient time on strategy:

1. Shortage of time.

2. The understanding of strategy is so inconsistent among employees and functional areas that it's difficult to even get started.

3. Strategy is considered the domain of only one or two top executives.

4. No uniform, methodical processes or frameworks are in place to facilitate strategy conversations and development, so it becomes time consuming and unproductive.

5. The strategy development process has not been successfully linked to daily activities, so the benefits aren't truly realized.

Let's address each of these issues individually:

1. **Time Shortage:** Wading through the daily swamp of e-mail, voice mail, meetings, and other activities can leave us gasping for time. Strategy development requires designated, unmovable periods of time on the calendar in order to receive the attention required to provide valuable direction.

2. **Misunderstanding the Concept of Strategy:** Organizations are made up of individuals coming from a host of different companies and educational backgrounds, so it's no wonder why there isn't universal understanding of an abstract concept like strategy. We provide educational courses for almost every topic imaginable—marketing, finance, diversity, leadership, etc.—but few, if any, for strategy. Put your employees through strategy training workshops.

3. **Strategy is the Domain of a Few:** Everyone can and should contribute to an organization's strategy, whether it be in the form of passing along competitive intelligence, receiving customer input, or coming up with new ideas for product enhancements. Strategic thinking is everyone's responsibility.

4. **No Strategy Processes are in Place:** We've all been in those rambling three-hour discussions that veer off course into business oblivion and leave those meetings wondering what we just talked about. Having a proven, methodical process for discussing strategy transforms wasted meetings into productive ones.

5. **Strategy is not Linked to Daily Work:** It's popular in today's business arena to say that "execution is everything"—"bad strategy well-executed is better than great strategy poorly

executed" is the mantra. However, consider this: you can have the highest performance Ferrari in the world (great execution) but if you're driving that Ferrari on a road headed over a cliff (poor strategy), you are finished.

Great strategy and great execution are not mutually exclusive. While one of the biggest challenges most companies face is successfully translating strategy into daily activities, you can use several tools and techniques to do so. We will review a simple two-page framework called the StrategyPrint® later in the book that will enable you to marry great strategy with great execution every time.

"...And Strategy For All"

Using a disciplined process to shape strategy at the division, business unit, product category, or brand level is extremely productive in setting direction and ensuring that the group is maximizing its business potential at all key points. In addition to the marketing and sales groups, it's beneficial for the other functional areas (IT, R&D, manufacturing, etc.) to utilize strategic thinking tools and the strategy development process to guide their contribution to the overall organization.

If you're still wondering whether your group needs a strategy development process, take the strategy process quiz.

STRATEGY PROCESS QUIZ

1. Does your group have a clear statement of strategy?   Y ❏ N ❏
2. Can everyone describe that strategy in one or two sentences?   Y ❏ N ❏
3. Is the strategy in written form?   Y ❏ N ❏
4. Does the strategy clearly differentiate you from competitors?   Y ❏ N ❏
5. Does your strategy serve as a guide to what *not* to do?   Y ❏ N ❏
6. Is the strategy comprised of a system of activities?   Y ❏ N ❏
7. Do you have effective methods and tools for communicating strategy throughout the company?   Y ❏ N ❏
8. Does the strategic plan drive daily activities?   Y ❏ N ❏
9. Is the plan a living document and updated regularly to remain useful?   Y ❏ N ❏
10. Do you have a strategy development process in place?   Y ❏ N ❏
11. Are your revenue growth and profitability meeting target expectations?   Y ❏ N ❏
12. Are you taking significant business away from your competitors?   Y ❏ N ❏
13. Are you capturing as much of your current customers' business as you would like?   Y ❏ N ❏
14. Are all the members of the management team trained in strategic thinking and able to contribute to strategy development?   Y ❏ N ❏
15. Does the group conduct strategic thinking and strategic planning sessions separately?   Y ❏ N ❏
16. Is the strategy development process facilitated by someone who can bring an objective perspective and is not affected by internal politics?   Y ❏ N ❏
17. Do you have a strategic filter for making resource allocation decisions?   Y ❏ N ❏
18. Do you have your purpose (mission, vision, and values statements) in writing?   Y ❏ N ❏
19. Are the different functional groups (marketing, sales, R&D) all working by the same strategy?   Y ❏ N ❏
20. Are you confident in the company's strategic direction?   Y ❏ N ❏

Scoring: 1 point for each "yes"   Total: Y_____

20 – 18: Strategically sound—crystal clear direction
17 – 15: Some degree of strategic ambiguity—on the verge of great success
14 – 12: Strategic drift—lack of clear strategy causes the group to be reactive and uncertain
  < 12: Driven by tactics and operations—time for a rethink

Strategy Defined

As strategy is an abstract concept that cannot be seen or touched, it has become a misunderstood catch-all term for everything under the business sun, including goals, objectives, mission, vision, metrics, and especially tactics. So how exactly do we create something that we cannot see or touch in order to guide and grow our business? We start with a common understanding of what strategy is, and what separates robust strategy from poor strategy.

Since taking over as CEO of Home Depot, Bob Nardelli has increased revenues 42% to $65 billion and profits 67% to $4.3 billion. In discussing his approach to strategy, Mr. Nardelli said,

> *The learning here is: lay a strategy, lay a course, and stay with it. Not blindly stay with it, but believe in it and mobilize, and do two of the most important things: make resource allocations into physical capital and human capital. And when you do that, it is amazing what happens.[4]*

In this statement, Mr. Nardelli captures the central premise of strategy—resource allocation. I define strategy as:

> *The intelligent allocation of limited resources through a unique system of activities to outperform the competition.*

We can simplify the definition even further into the three A's of strategy (Figure 1.0).

Figure 1.0 Three A's of Strategy

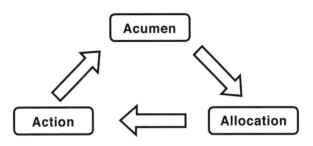

Acumen: Business insights generated by strategic thinking

Allocation: Deciding where and in what proportion to place resources

Action: Maintaining the discipline to execute the activities of the strategy

When we break strategy down into the three A's, we are putting flesh onto the abstract skeleton of strategy. Even so, the terms "goals," "objectives," "strategies," and "tactics" (G.O.S.T.) are often used interchangeably. Let's take a moment to review each for clarity's sake.

- **Goal:** A general target—What *generally* you are trying to achieve.

- **Objective:** Specific outcome desired—What *specifically* you are trying to achieve.

  The acronym SMART provides a helpful reminder for the criteria of an objective:
  Specific
  Measurable
  Achievable
  Relevant
  Time-bound

- **Strategy:** The resource allocation plan—How *generally* to achieve the goals/objectives.

- **Tactic:** The tangible activities/items that carry out the strategies—How *specifically* to achieve the goals/objectives.

Goals and objectives are *what* we are trying to accomplish. Strategies and tactics are *how* we will accomplish them. The key differences can be represented in Figure 1.1.

Figure 1.1 G.O.S.T. Summary

Goal	Objective	Strategy	Tactic
What	What	How	How
Generally	Specifically	Generally	Specifically

Since strategy and tactics both address the *how,* they are often used interchangeably. A helpful way to remember the differences between the two is the "Rule of Touch." If you can physically reach out and touch it, it is most likely a tactic (sales brochure, CD-ROM, direct mail piece, etc.). If you can't physically touch it (leveraging a specialty sales force with a single product focus), it is most likely a strategy. This is in sync with our analogy of strategy development and "sculpting air." As Chinese General and Philosopher Sun Tzu noted, "All the men can see the tactics I use to conquer, but what none can see is the strategy out of which great victory is evolved."[5]

Michael Porter, professor at Harvard Business School, gives us another simple way to think about strategy. He describes strategy as performing different activities from competitors or performing similar activities in a different manner.[6] An example of a company that used a different activity as its strategy is Peapod. When they first entered the market, they provided a different activity for shopping: bringing groceries to customers instead of having customers go to a grocery store. This differentiated activity comprised a distinct strategy.

Strategy can also be described as performing similar activities to competitors in a different manner. Southwest Airlines took a similar activity—flying people from Point A to Point B, and they've done it differently than competitors, such as United Airlines and American Airlines. They've performed this similar activity in a number of different ways that has increased their efficiency and reduced their costs, such as not serving food on flights, not issuing assigned seats, not using the hub and spoke model, and so on. This allows them to perform the similar activity of air travel in a different and more successful way.

This latter perspective becomes helpful when we use it as a lens to view our business planning efforts. At face value, a number of our activities or tactics aren't entirely different from those the competition employs. However, if we can find ways to create differentiation within and around the tactic, we can begin developing a differentiated strategy.

Operational Effectiveness

Operational effectiveness is the proverbial wolf in strategy's clothing. It's the concept most commonly confused with strategy. Operational effectiveness is performing similar activities in a similar manner to competitors.[7] By employing operational effectiveness without strategy, we are in effect saying that we are going to run the exact same race as our competitors and hope to be a little faster. Incorporating strategy indicates that we are going to run a different course than our competitors—one in which we've set ourselves up to win.

Look at nearly any industry and you'll see examples of established companies locked in battles of operational effectiveness. When companies become complacent and rely on doing the same things in the same ways as their competitors (i.e., United Airlines and American Airlines), differentiated entrants come into the marketplace and begin taking their business (i.e., Southwest Airlines and JetBlue Airlines).

Three Criteria of Robust Strategy

Now that we have a common understanding of strategy and key planning terms, let's take a look at the three criteria that separate a good strategy from a poor one.

1. **Differentiation:** Distinction from the competition
2. **Focus:** Making trade-offs to allocate resources
3. **System:** Creating an activity network

Differentiation

Differentiation for competitive advantage in business has its roots in science. In 1934 a Moscow University researcher named G.F. Gause, known as the "father of mathematical biology," published the results of a set of experiments. In those experiments, he placed two small animals (protozoans) of the same genus in a bottle with an ample supply of food. If the animals were of the same genus and a different species, they could survive and persist together. If the animals were of the same genus and the same species, they could not survive and persist together. These results led to the Principle of Competitive Exclusion: "No two species can coexist that make their living in the identical way."[8]

Open the newspaper and read about the companies that are struggling and it's a good bet that one of the reasons for their struggles is their failure to pay heed to the Principle of Competitive Exclusion. They are stuck doing the same things in the same way as their competition. Jeffrey Immelt, Chairman and CEO of GE, has said, "GE must look different…act different…be different…to excel in the years ahead."[9] Notice that he didn't say GE must be "better." He specifically chose the word "different" and used it three times to emphasize his company's understanding that the road to success in business is paved by differentiation from the competition. We will examine a number of tools later in the book to help you identify and leverage your differentiation in the marketplace.

Focus

Focus demands that we have the discipline to allocate resources to specific areas and activities and not spread them evenly across the business. Focus comes from the ability and willingness to make trade-offs. Trade-offs are about choosing one path and not the other. Trade-offs involve incompatible activities—more of one thing necessitates less of another. In the pharmaceutical industry, one can choose to be the leader in research and development or the leading provider of low-cost drugs, but cannot do both without bearing major inefficiencies.

Making trade-offs is one of the most difficult tasks for most managers, and the result is that they never do make the necessary trade-offs. Instead, they hedge their bets and abide by the adage of "trying to be everything to everyone." Harvard Business School professor Michael Porter has said, "The essence of strategy is in choosing what not to do. Without trade-offs, there would be no need for choice and thus no need for strategy. Any good idea could and would be quickly imitated."

Three sets of questions can help us begin the process of identifying the trade-offs for our business:

Who are we serving?	Who are we not serving?
What are we offering?	What are we not offering?
How are we offering it?	How will it not be offered?

Most managers do a relatively good job of answering the questions in the left column. What most managers don't do is take the time to answer the questions in the right column—the ones that determine the "nots"—the things we are not going to do. As strategy involves "the intelligent allocation of *limited* resources…," choosing where not to allocate resources is a critical step in the development of strong strategy.

Meg Whitman, CEO of eBay, explains the crucial role focus played in the successful development of the company:

The key decisions can all be characterized by focus, focus, focus. Back in March 1998, we were faced with a decision on what categories we wanted to focus on. We decided to really be a collectibles company. The heaviest users were collectors, the heaviest sellers were collectors. It was a very explicit strategic decision, because part of the group wanted to go into consumer electronics and all of these other categories we are in today. And we answered, "We have only a limited number of resources. What is the best focus that we can have?[10]

Ms. Whitman realized early on that good strategy involves the discipline to focus one's limited resources on the key areas that will fuel success.

Here are the four reasons why the majority of organizations don't focus their resources through strategy:

1. **Unclear purpose:** Working without a clearly articulated purpose in the form of a mission, vision, or values statement is like a rudderless ship. It floats along, being pushed by competitors and circumstances into all kinds of strange places—places that waste precious time and resources.

2. **Lack of business intelligence:** Not taking the time for strategic thinking, which involves methodically and comprehensively assessing the market, customers, competitors, and the organization, inhibits the ability to focus. Without the generation of business intelligence, resource allocation is a crapshoot.

3. **Action orientation:** As we are now all technologically tethered to one another and expected to be "on" 24/7, activity is the name of the game. Focusing resources requires us to periodically step back out of the fray and thoughtfully assess the situation. A good strategist isn't driven by the calendar or the clock—they're driven by those few things that make a difference in their business.

4. **Unwillingness to make trade-offs:** Focus requires trade-offs and trade-offs require calculated risk. Spreading resources and not focusing allows us to reduce our vulnerability and lower the risk. However, just like financial investing, the more we reduce risk, the more we reduce the chance for great financial success.

System

While a strategy can be made up of only one activity, there are compelling reasons for building an activity system to drive your strategy. As the number of activities comprising your strategy increases, it becomes more and more difficult for competitors to emulate the entire system of strategy. This premise is evident in Figure 1.2.[11]

Figure 1.2 Arithmetic Support of System of Activities

# of Activities	Numerical Representation	Probability of competitor match
1	.9	90%
2	.9 x .9	81%
3	.9 x .9 x .9	73%
4	.9 x .9 x .9 x .9	66%
10	$.9^{10}$	35%

In this figure, we can see that the probability of a competitor successfully copying a strategy involving only one activity is relatively high at 90% or .9. With three activities comprising our strategy, the probability of a competitor successfully emulating the strategy drops to 73%. Creating a system of strategy involving ten activities significantly diminishes the competitor's ability to follow our lead. Later in the book we will introduce a tool called the Activity System Map, which will enable you to create a system of strategic activities.

DIFFERENCE MAKERS

- Strategy development can be likened to sculpting, both of which require the vision to foresee the finished form and the skill, insight, and craftsmanship to create it. We use the term "sculpting air" to capture the challenge of creating something that we cannot see—strategy.

- Research has shown that all financially successful companies excel at strategy development and execution.

- A study by the Economist Intelligence Unit showed that senior executives are only spending 15% of their time together on strategic issues.

- Strategy is defined as "the intelligent allocation of limited resources through a unique system of activities to outperform the competition."

- Strategy is comprised of the three A's:
  1. Acumen: Business insights generated by strategic thinking
  2. Allocation: Deciding where and in what proportion to place resources
  3. Action: Maintaining the discipline to execute the activities of the strategy

- A goal is a general target—What *generally* you are trying to achieve.

Continued on next page

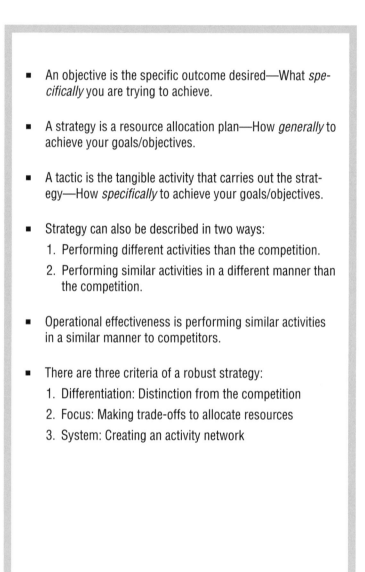

- An objective is the specific outcome desired—What *specifically* you are trying to achieve.

- A strategy is a resource allocation plan—How *generally* to achieve your goals/objectives.

- A tactic is the tangible activity that carries out the strategy—How *specifically* to achieve your goals/objectives.

- Strategy can also be described in two ways:
  1. Performing different activities than the competition.
  2. Performing similar activities in a different manner than the competition.

- Operational effectiveness is performing similar activities in a similar manner to competitors.

- There are three criteria of a robust strategy:
  1. Differentiation: Distinction from the competition
  2. Focus: Making trade-offs to allocate resources
  3. System: Creating an activity network

CHAPTER 2

Shaping Strategy

Now imagine someone crafting strategy...
Craft evokes traditional skill, dedication,
perfection through the mastery of detail...a feeling
of intimacy and harmony with the materials at
hand...Formulation and implementation merge
into a fluid process of learning, through which
creative strategies evolve.

– Henry Mintzberg
Professor, McGill University

With the breakneck speed of today's economy, it is fashionable to say that strategic planning is no longer useful. Things change so rapidly that taking time to think about and craft strategy is simply not possible. However, research has shown just the opposite is true. A study of more than 100 companies showed that 70% of successful business ventures originated from a process of strategic planning, while 20% were opportunistic and 10% of an undisclosed origin.[1]

There are seven primary benefits of a strategy development process:

1. **Establishes direction**—focuses everyone's activities into cohesive plans to achieve the group's goals.
2. **Stimulates innovation**—forces the challenging of assumptions and sacred cows while discovering new insights.
3. **Improves decision making**—provides sound, consistent criteria to help managers effectively allocate resources.
4. **Enables trans-silo communication**—breaks down the barriers that often exist between functional units in the organization through the sharing of perspectives.
5. **Creates prepared minds**—requires managers to take a holistic view of the business by methodically studying the market, customers, competitors, and the organization.
6. **Instills confident purpose**—gives employees a deeper sense of meaning about their work.
7. **Increases revenue, profitability, and productivity**—promotes profitable growth by ensuring that resources are invested in more of the right activities and less of the wrong activities.

As Tim Brown, President and CEO of Ideo, said, "By building your strategy early on, in a sense you're doing a premortem. You're giving yourself a chance to uncover problems and fix them in real time, as the strategy unfolds."[2]

To create a best-of-breed strategy development process, research was conducted on more than 75 different systems utilized by the premier corporations, management consultancies, and universities around the world. Interviews with dozens of senior executives ranging from *Fortune* 100 companies to start-up firms were conducted to determine the most important criteria in a strategy development process and the expected outputs.

From the primary research with senior executives, it was determined that a best-of-breed process meets three criteria:

1. **Simple**—the process must be understandable, manageable, and easy to implement.
2. **Concise**—the process must be clear and succinct.
3. **Effective**—the process must provide a tangible output that drives daily activity and improves performance on key metrics.

The research also showed that a best-of-breed strategy development process would yield the following outputs:

1. **Transparency** of key business insights across the different functional units.
2. **Strategic filters** that improve decision making and resource allocation.
3. **List of critical issues** to frame the management team's work.
4. **Strategic action plan** that guides and profitably grows the business.
5. **Optimal positioning** of the company, product, or service for competitive advantage.
6. **Focus and unity of effort** across the organization on the key success factors.

The result of the primary and secondary research was the design of a best-of-breed strategy development process that includes five phases (Figure 2.0).

Figure 2.0 The Process of Shaping Strategy

The Strategy Shaping Process

The process of developing strategy is quite similar to the process that a sculptor uses to create a work of art. Therefore, we describe the five phases of the best-of-breed strategy development process in concert with the five phases of sculpting.

I. Discovery—"Choosing the Tools"

A sculptor begins the process by selecting the material to work with (clay, marble, metal) and the appropriate tools (hammer, chisel, knives) with which to work. Similarly, the discovery phase of strategy development involves the selection of the people, process, and information to be used.

The discovery phase entails the designation of the strategy development team, an outline of the process being used, and pre-work. The pre-work involves intelligence gathering on the market, customers, competitors, and the organization, including primary research with customers and employees in the form of one-to-one interviews or focus groups.

II. Strategic Thinking—"Playing in Space"

Once a sculptor has chosen the tools, she begins working ideas out in space by creating a maquette, or small 3-D model of the intended work. The strategic thinking phase provides the forum for the group to begin generating and capturing their business insights in model format.

The strategic thinking sessions, conducted with the strategy development team, are designed to generate insights through a methodical and comprehensive examination of the four key areas of the business:

1. Market
2. Customers
3. Competitors
4. Organization

III. Strategic Planning—"Building the Framework"

After creating the miniature 3-D model, the sculptor working in clay creates a skeletal structure or wire frame, known as an armature, to serve as the foundation of the sculpture. The strategic planning phase acts in the same manner, creating the framework for the strategy and all of its elements.

The strategic planning phase transforms the insights generated from strategic thinking into the strategic action plan

(StrategyPrint®) that achieves the organization's goals and objectives and includes the appropriate timelines and budgets.

IV. Strategy Rollout—"Sculpting the Masterpiece"

Once the framework has been developed, the artist sculpts the figure, adding and taking away material as necessary. In the same way, the strategy rollout phase transforms the strategic plan into the activities and offerings that move the business forward.

The strategy rollout phase ensures that the key elements of the strategic action plan are clearly communicated throughout the organization and that an implementation plan is in place. The following steps support the strategy rollout:

1. Development of the communication plan.
2. Dissemination of the strategic action plan through the chosen communication vehicles to employees.
3. Collection and review of feedback regarding the strategic action plan components and the effectiveness of their communication to the organization.
4. Incorporation and application of the strategic action plan to employees' daily activities and their corresponding metrics.
5. Periodic pulse-taking to monitor progress and assess effectiveness and relevance of both strategy and tactics and their understanding by employees.

V. Strategy Tune-up—"Polishing the Form"

Once the sculptor finishes the work, she must ensure that adjustments, such as proper lighting, and maintenance activities, including cleaning and polishing, are performed on a regular basis to keep the sculpture in its best form. Similarly, the strategy tune-up phase serves to keep the strategy evergreen.

Comprised of a half to one day session on a quarterly basis, the strategy tune-up consists of periodic formal reviews of the business by the strategy development team to hone their work. The team methodically reviews the four key areas of the business to identify changes and make any necessary adjustments to strategy and tactics.

The StrategySphere System®

The best-of-breed strategy development process is called the StrategySphere System. It is a systemic process of analysis and synthesis that generates business insights that lead to a focused set of actionable strategies. The name "StrategySphere" is symbolic of the continuous cycle involved in shaping strategy as represented by the endless form of a sphere. The descriptor "System" reflects the interacting, interrelated, and interdependent elements (market, customers, competitors, etc.) that form the complex nature of a business. The Strategy-Sphere System's five phases and their individual components are represented in Figure 2.1.

The StrategySphere System includes only those elements of strategy development that have been proven valuable in shaping strategy. The paradoxical beauty of the system is that it is both comprehensive and concise—elements can be used or not used depending on where the group is in their strategy development efforts. So while a start-up company may need to cover all of the elements listed in the StrategySphere System, a seasoned division of a large company may only choose certain areas to augment the information and insights they already have. The ability to customize the strategy development

Figure 2.1 The StrategySphere System®

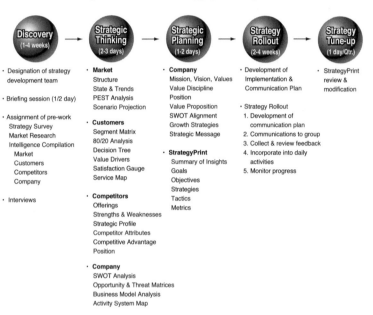

process for a specific company, business unit, or product team ensures maximum productivity at a minimum cost.

Another advantage of the system is that the entire process can be completed with a flipchart and markers. All of the models that will be covered in the strategic thinking and strategic planning phases can be created by hand during the strategy development sessions. A more advanced option is to utilize the proprietary software system for instant creation of the models and a database to store the insights and information generated upon their completion. Either way, this book will provide you with all of the tools necessary to effectively shape strategy for your group.

DIFFERENCE MAKERS

- Benefits of a strategy development process:
  1. Establishes direction—focuses everyone's activities into cohesive plans to achieve the group's goals.
  2. Stimulates innovation—forces the challenging of assumptions and sacred cows while discovering new insights.
  3. Improves decision making—provides sound, consistent criteria to help managers effectively allocate resources.
  4. Enables trans-silo communication—breaks down the barriers that often exist between functional units in the organization through the sharing of perspectives.
  5. Creates prepared minds—requires managers to take a holistic view of the business by methodically studying the market, customers, competitors and the organization.
  6. Instills confident purpose—gives employees a deeper sense of meaning about their work.
  7. Increases revenue, profitability, and productivity—promotes profitable growth by ensuring that resources are invested in more of the right activities and less of the wrong activities.

- Research from interviews with senior executives shows that a strong strategy development process meets three criteria:
  1. Simple—the process must be understandable, manageable, and easy to implement.
  2. Concise—the process must be clear and succinct.

Continued on next page

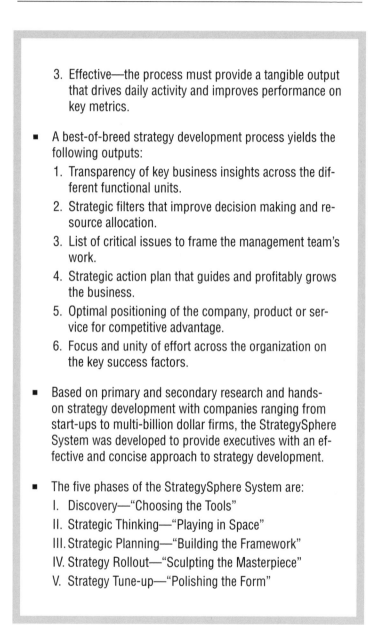

3. Effective—the process must provide a tangible output that drives daily activity and improves performance on key metrics.

- A best-of-breed strategy development process yields the following outputs:
    1. Transparency of key business insights across the different functional units.
    2. Strategic filters that improve decision making and resource allocation.
    3. List of critical issues to frame the management team's work.
    4. Strategic action plan that guides and profitably grows the business.
    5. Optimal positioning of the company, product or service for competitive advantage.
    6. Focus and unity of effort across the organization on the key success factors.

- Based on primary and secondary research and hands-on strategy development with companies ranging from start-ups to multi-billion dollar firms, the StrategySphere System was developed to provide executives with an effective and concise approach to strategy development.

- The five phases of the StrategySphere System are:
    I. Discovery—"Choosing the Tools"
    II. Strategic Thinking—"Playing in Space"
    III. Strategic Planning—"Building the Framework"
    IV. Strategy Rollout—"Sculpting the Masterpiece"
    V. Strategy Tune-up—"Polishing the Form"

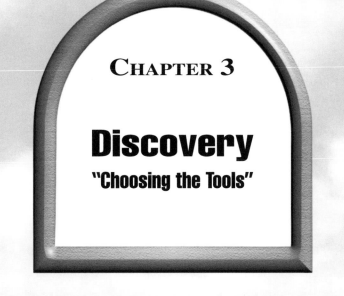

CHAPTER 3

Discovery
"Choosing the Tools"

*Discovery consists of seeing what everybody has
seen and thinking what nobody has thought.*

– Albert von Szent-Gyorgyi
Nobel Prize-Winning Biochemist

Just as the sculptor must first select the appropriate materials and tools with which to work, the executive must select the people, process, and information to be used. The discovery phase is the initiation of the strategy development process. Done well, it provides the mental fuel to challenge assumptions, mine for insights, and generate momentum. Done poorly, it stifles growth by not allowing the organization to fully realize its potential.

The discovery phase begins with the acknowledgment that developing better strategy is important to the organization's long-term growth. In some companies this realization never takes place, never gets acted upon, or both. The result is Bumper-Car Strategy. The company reacts to everything it bumps into (competitor price cuts, unprofitable customers, meaningless market trends, etc.) and spins frenetically with no discernible course of action. Meanwhile, managers frantically try to turn the inoperable steering wheel.

When the decision is made to invest in developing strategy, the company takes the following steps:

1. Designation of the strategy development team leader.
2. Selection of the strategy development team members.
3. Briefing session to orient the strategy development team and prepare for the process.
4. Assignment and completion of pre-work.
5. Interviews with employees, customers, and non-customers.

Getting Started

The first step is to select a strategy development team leader to guide the team through the process. This is a crucial decision because an ineffective strategy development team leader can derail the entire process, resulting in poor strategy, unproductive meetings, wasted time, deflated morale, and a loss in confidence by the management team or Board of Directors. Companies have several options for the position of strategy development team leader. Those options, along with their advantages and disadvantages, are summarized below:

Senior Executive

A senior executive brings a tremendous amount of company and industry knowledge and intimately knows the management team members. Due to their extensive day-to-day responsibilities, they may face challenges in finding time to orchestrate, facilitate, and lead the strategy development process. They may unintentionally inhibit candid conversation because of their position and authority relative to the other team members. If they are in a functional role such as marketing, R&D, sales, etc., they will naturally bring that mental frame and its corresponding preferences to the objective role of facilitator. If the executive is in an internal strategy role, they can be of great value in assessing the strategy content that's discussed. However, their ability to provide valuable input on strategy content is severely compromised by the conflicting task of being an objective facilitator because the two roles inherently require different positions.

General Trainer/Facilitator

A general trainer/facilitator may be an employee or outside resource. Skill in facilitating meetings and not bringing a specific functional perspective are both positives in generating conversation. The lack of expertise in the area of strategy that goes along with a general training background may impede their ability to provide objective and insightful feedback on the quality of responses and output generated during meetings. Without a deep background in strategy, they may not have knowledge of the full spectrum of tools and frameworks that fit with the appropriate strategic context of the business.

Independent Strategist

The independent strategist's expertise in the subject of strategy and their skill and experience facilitating the strategy development process ensures that the process is effectively and efficiently managed to produce the optimal outcome.

The objectivity that comes with their position as a third-party resource allows them to honestly assess feedback and push sensitive subjects without fear of political repercussions. The ability to competently assess input and participant responses is high because of their "been there, done that" portfolio of experience and strategy expertise. A potential downside is the investment in up-front costs to bring in an expert.

Once the company has made a decision about who the strategy development team leader will be, the process of shaping strategy can be designed according to the company's specific needs. One of the team leader's key roles will be selecting the appropriate sections and exercises from the full menu of strategic thinking models. The proper decision on which elements to use ensures that the process is as simple, concise, and effective as possible.

Designation of Team

The strategy development team should be carefully selected to ensure functional diversity, content knowledge, and strategic thinking skill sets. Functional diversity means that the relevant functional units (marketing, sales, R&D, operations, HR, finance, etc.) are represented to provide various perspectives. By including key representatives from the appropriate areas, a greater level of "buy-in" will occur since they have all had the opportunity to provide input. This increased level of "buy-in" will result in more effective execution of the strategy since the representatives have publicly committed themselves to the outcome.

All of the members of the strategy development team should be regarded as highly knowledgeable about the company's offerings so that all of the relevant products and services are represented. Finally, team members should have a track record of being considered strong strategic thinkers. A strong strategic thinker has demonstrated the mental agility to take a holistic view of the business, be a proficient decision maker, innovatively solve problems, and effectively lead their groups.

The size of the strategy development team can vary and is often relative to the size of the organization. Generally, smaller organizations where executives wear multiple hats and that have one or two products will have fewer team members than large global companies with hundreds of products, because fewer representatives are needed. To provide a rule-of-thumb, small organizations (< $100 million in revenue) will have 5-7 members, mid-sized organizations ($100 million – $1 billion in revenue) will have 7-10 members, and large organizations (>$1 billion in revenue) will have 10-15 members. For developing strategy at the division, business unit, or product levels, teams should consist of only those representative stakeholders that have a direct connection to the strategy and its execution.

Briefing Session

The team leader holds a half to one day briefing session with all the members of the strategy development team. The briefing session is designed to welcome team members, convey the importance of their task, educate them on the strategy development process, and assign pre-work to be completed prior to the strategic thinking phase.

The welcoming comments should come from the most senior position represented to emphasize the importance of the process to the team. The senior executive should clearly articulate the benefits of the strategy development process and how it will positively affect the organization. They can then introduce the strategy development team leader and have them facilitate the remainder of the session.

The team leader should walk the team members through the steps of the strategy development process. It's always helpful to use a visual diagram to explain the process so that the team can see the entire process in advance.

To maximize the time spent in the strategic thinking sessions, it is necessary to compile and extract all the relevant primary and secondary information available with some form of institutional information audit. A good deal of this information may already exist, such as market research with customers, market analyses, competitive intelligence, and so on. If the information does not exist, depending on time and budget considerations, a short-list of the must-have information can be developed. The intelligence compilation should have information categorized in the areas of market, customers, competitors, and the company to simplify its use later in the process.

In addition to this information, the strategy development team members should complete a Strategy Survey that focuses their thinking on the critical areas of the business and begins preparing them for the strategic thinking sessions. It's important to have team members fill out the Strategy Survey individually. Research has shown that brainstorming individually *prior* to group discussion is always more productive in both the quality and quantity of thinking than group brainstorming. The Strategy Survey contains five sections of questions for consideration:

1. Market
2. Customers
3. Competitors
4. Company
5. Strategy

On the following pages is a sample of questions that may be used in the Strategy Survey.

The Strategy Survey is an effective tool in stimulating the strategy development team's thinking prior to the group sessions and makes those sessions more productive. Be sure to include the Strategy Survey in your strategy development process to "prime the pump" and begin capturing the insights that will fuel your plan.

Interviews

Time permitting, it is valuable to conduct primary research with customers, competitor's customers, and your own employees to ensure that you are using multiple lenses to view the business. These interviews are intended to solicit information, insights, and perceptions of the business from people holding different positions than those members of the strategy development team. In effect, the interviews serve to add a reality check to the group's discussions by balancing the team's expertise with the direct observations of customers, competitor's customers, and employees.

While it is less time consuming to do phone or mail interviews, it is always valuable to conduct individual face-to-face interviews to allow for in-depth probing into "hot button" areas. Face-to-face interviews also allow for assessment of body language, tone of voice, and general interest levels regarding the subjects covered in the questions.

SAMPLE OF THE STRATEGY SURVEY

Market

- What is the current state of the market? (check one & complete rate)

  Growing ❏   Stable ❏   Declining ❏   Rate: ___%

- What is the market structure? (check low, medium, or high for each)

Barriers to entry	Low ❏	Medium ❏	High ❏
Power of customers	Low ❏	Medium ❏	High ❏
Power of suppliers	Low ❏	Medium ❏	High ❏
Threat of substitutes	Low ❏	Medium ❏	High ❏
Industry competition	Low ❏	Medium ❏	High ❏

Customers

- How do you add value to the customer?

- List the top three customer value drivers and rate your company versus your best competitor on a scale of 1-10, with 1 being low ability to meet value and 10 being high ability to meet value:

  Primary customer group: _____

Customer value drivers	My Score	My Best Competitor's Score
1. _____	_____	_____
2. _____	_____	_____
3. _____	_____	_____

Competitors

- Who are your most dangerous competitors? Why?

- Name your top three competitors and the three points of differentiation for each from your customer's perspective.

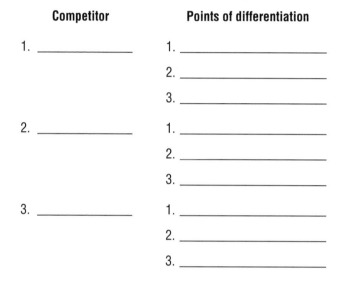

Competitor	Points of differentiation
1. _____	1. _____
	2. _____
	3. _____
2. _____	1. _____
	2. _____
	3. _____
3. _____	1. _____
	2. _____
	3. _____

Company

- What is the organization's purpose?

- What are the organization's core competencies?

Strategy

- What criteria are used for resource allocation?

- What is the company's profit model (how do you make money)?

- How do you communicate strategy throughout the organization?

A standard questionnaire similar in structure and content to the Strategy Survey should be used and the interviewing responsibilities distributed evenly among the members of the strategy development team. Having the team members conduct the interviews themselves adds a richness and texture to their understanding of the business that further enhances the group's input during the strategic thinking and planning phases.

DIFFERENCE MAKERS

- The strategy development process begins with the discovery phase.

- The discovery phase consists of five steps:
  1. Designation of the strategy development team leader.
  2. Selection of the strategy development team members.
  3. Briefing session to orient the strategy development team and prepare for the process.
  4. Assignment and completion of pre-work.
  5. Interviews with employees, customers, and non-customers.

- Utilizing an independent strategy expert to serve as the strategy development team leader provides the following benefits:
  - Ensures that the process is effectively managed to produce the optimal outcome.
  - Provides the most efficient use of internal resources as it enables executives to focus on their day-to-day responsibilities.
  - Brings objectivity with their position as a third-party resource external to the company, allowing them to honestly assess feedback and push on sensitive subjects without fear of political consequences.
  - The ability to competently assess input and participant responses is high because of their "been there, done that" portfolio of experience from working with a range of companies and the expertise that comes from their laser-like focus on the strategy development process.

Continued on next page

- The size of the strategy development team is relative to the size of the organization. To provide a rule-of-thumb, small organizations (< $100 million in revenue) will have 5-7 members, mid-sized organizations ($100 million - $1 billion in revenue) will have 7-10 members, and large organizations (>$1 billion in revenue) will have 10-15 members.

- To maximize the time spent in the strategic thinking sessions it is necessary to compile and extract all the relevant primary and secondary information available. A good deal of this information may already exist, such as market research with customers, market analyses, competitive intelligence, etc.

- The strategy development team members should complete a Strategy Survey that focuses their thinking on the critical areas of the business and begins preparing them for the strategic thinking sessions.

- The Strategy Survey prepares the strategy development team members for the strategic thinking sessions by focusing their attention on the key areas of the business:
  1. Market
  2. Customers
  3. Competitors
  4. Company
  5. Strategy

- It is valuable to conduct primary research with customers, competitor's customers, and your own employees to ensure that you are using multiple lenses to view your business.

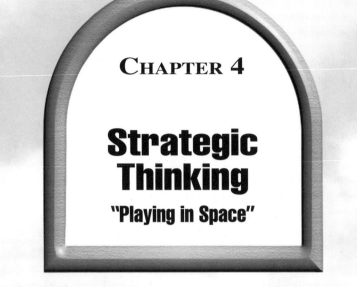

CHAPTER 4

Strategic Thinking
"Playing in Space"

*In strategic thinking, one first seeks a clear
understanding of the particular character of each
element of a situation and then makes the fullest
possible use of human brain power to restructure
the elements in the most advantageous way.*

– Keniche Ohmae
Business Strategist

When creating something from nothing, as all works of
art do, the sculptor first shapes the figure in her mind.
Without first visualizing the sculpture, the artist is destined
to merely recreate past works. In the same fashion, omitting
the strategic thinking phase from the strategy development
process condemns organizations to "more of the same." They
inadvertently move from compiling market research and com-

petitive intelligence (discovery phase) directly to strategic planning.

Big mistake.

The strategic thinking phase is crucial because it offers the opportunity to challenge assumptions, spark innovation, and catalyze the insights that will drive future success. Foregoing the strategic thinking phase will almost certainly allow entrenched institutional assumptions and sacred cows to take over, thereby invalidating the process almost before it begins. Skipping the strategic thinking phase and moving directly from discovery to strategic planning is tantamount to an organizational lobotomy because the thinking function has been excised.

The intelligence gathered during the discovery phase on the market, customers, competitors, and the company is used as the fuel for the strategic thinking phase. All the information collected is summarized and disseminated to strategy team members and used to populate the strategic thinking models. The strategic thinking phase is designed to generate business insights. The strategic planning phase then channels those insights into an action plan to most effectively allocate resources to meet the company's goals and objectives.

Generally, two to three days is an appropriate period of time for the strategy development team to spend in the strategic thinking phase when developing strategy for an organization. One to two days may be more appropriate for a business unit or product team. In my experience facilitating the strategy development process for organizations, once you move the group past three continuous days, the quality of thinking deteriorates and burnout sets in.

The strategic thinking sessions will be the most mentally draining exercises the team will go through. The sessions will stimulate vigorous, if not heated debate, as the team members come to the realization that what they thought were common assumptions and perspectives are not necessarily shared by all. However, these sessions will also be the most rewarding because they create alignment around a unified direction.

Research has shown that strategic thinking is comprised of skill sets that can be practiced for improvement. Areas such as decision making, problem solving, discovering purpose, modeling, and systems thinking all contribute to a person's ability to think strategically.

Strategic thinking is certainly not limited to a phase in the strategy development process. On the contrary, it is a skill set that your entire organization should be working to develop and practice on a daily basis. World-class organizations understand the urgency in providing training and tools for their managers to become more effective strategists.

For example, the article "GE's Next Workout. The Industrial Giant's Legendary Learning Center, Crotonville, has a New Assignment: Teach Every Manager to be a Strategist," emphasizes the importance that GE is placing on having managers that are skilled at strategic thinking.[1] Bob Corcoran, director of Crotonville, said, "Jeff (Jeffrey Immelt, CEO of GE) inherited a company skilled at execution—one that can stop on a dime and deliver results. The company just loves to execute. Now the question is how to develop the top line."[2]

Coupled with their focus on strategic thinking is a renewed interest in strategy development:

> *The other shift relates to a new philosophy of strategy formulation. Mr. Immelt is instituting, for the first time since the early 1980s, a more formal strategic planning process at GE. Mr. Immelt is involving line managers in debates and dialogues about long-term strategy in which they talk through their perceptions of technological change and the business environment and envision the 'big wins' that might be possible over the next 15 years.*[3]

The article's author, Art Kleiner, concludes by saying, "If you bring smart people together regularly to step back from the day-to-day urgencies and improve their work, with a clear line of accountability for results afterward, it's amazing what can happen."[4] That is exactly the intent of the strategic thinking phase—to provide a forum for team members to step back, reflect, and use strategic thinking to generate business insights to guide and grow the business.

Visualizing Insights

Modeling is the platform on which the strategic thinking phase is built. Models provide a visual method of extracting the group's insights and capturing those insights in a tangible medium. As Immanuel Kant said, "Thinking in pictures precedes thinking in words."

In order to most effectively and efficiently harness the group's insights, the strategic thinking phase is categorized into four key areas of any business: market, customers, competitors, and company. Methodically moving through these four areas and utilizing the appropriate models within each ensures a comprehensive and meaningful examination of the business.

The remainder of the chapter will be divided into the four areas of the strategic thinking phase (market, customers, competitors, company). Three models will be discussed in each area for a total of twelve models in all. While there are nearly sixty models to choose from in the StrategySphere System, these twelve will give you an excellent base to stimulate the strategic thinking sessions. It is a critical responsibility of the strategy development team leader to ensure that the right models are chosen for the sessions based on the content and context of the business situation.

Strategic Thinking Models

Market	Customers	Competitors	Company
1. PEST Analysis 2. StructureScape 3. Five Forces of Competition	1. Customer Matrix 2. Service Map 3. Value Driver Matrix	1. Strategy Profile 2. Spider Map 3. Competitive Advantage	1. SWOT Analysis 2. Opportunity & Threat Matrices 3. Activity System Map

You may choose to simply skim through the twelve models contained in this chapter and move onto the elements of strategic planning (i.e., developing growth strategies, selecting a value discipline, competitive positioning, etc.) in Chapter Five. A brief review of the twelve models will give you a general idea of their application and you can then re-read this section more carefully when it comes time to select the appropriate models for the strategic thinking sessions.

A brief description of each model is accompanied by a graphical depiction to provide you with both the information and example necessary to apply it to your business. The models use the following three fictitious medical device companies to provide you with real-world examples:

- TechnoStar—the product leader based on innovative technology;
- CostAlert—the provider of the lowest cost products; and
- CustoSolution—developer of customized solutions.

These fictitious companies provide a representative makeup of the three primary types of entrants in any industry, enabling you to quickly and easily apply the models to your business.

MARKET

Strategic thinking about the market enables us to immerse ourselves in the context of the business. The context represents the circumstances within which the business operates. Jeffrey Immelt, Chairman and CEO of GE, wrote in a letter to shareholders the following: "The most important thing I've learned since becoming CEO is context. It's how your company fits in with the world and how you respond to it."[5] Comprehensive strategic thinking on the market enhances our ability to understand and leverage the context that our business operates in.

You can use the following three models to generate market insights:

1. PEST Analysis
2. StructureScape
3. Five Forces of Competition

PEST Analysis

A good place to begin the market review is with a discussion of the Political, Economic, Social, and Technological (PEST) factors influencing the business. These four categories will enable you to capture the key elements swirling about your business and better prepare for their effects.

The PEST Analysis shown in Figure 4.0 is for the medical device arena in which the three fictitious companies reside:

Figure 4.0 PEST Analysis

Political	Economic
1. Legislation on nurse-to-patient ratios 2. FDA mandated use of bar codes on products 3. Joint Commission requirements	1. Employers passing greater share of healthcare costs to employees 2. Retirement of Baby Boomers and their effect on Medicare 3. Group Purchasing Organization's power
Social	**Technological**
1. Heightened consumer knowledge of medical issues and treatment options 2. Media's negative portrayal of the healthcare industry 3. Publication of healthcare institution's success and failure rates	1. Industry moving toward Radio Frequency Identification technology 2. Institutions looking for connectivity between drugs, medical devices, monitoring systems and records 3. Preference for smaller, cross-platform devices

The PEST Analysis can be created by dividing the headings into four columns and placing the input under each. After the initial lists are developed, take time to go back and eliminate the factors that are not deemed significant in the overall scope of the business.

StructureScape

The StructureScape, originally developed by Dr. Milind Lele, is a method for plotting the size and influence of each of the market players relative to the market leader using market share, size, sales volume, etc.[6] It provides a snapshot of the market landscape and grounds the strategy development team in the reality of the business's position. It's all too common for a group of managers to say, "Our goal is to be the market leader within a year," without having objectively looked at the structure of the market to determine if that is indeed feasible. Working without the gravity of reality can be exhilarating but soon leads to asphyxiation. It's important at the outset to ground the team in an objective review of the market.

In Figure 4.1, we can see that TechnoStar is the market leader with a 37.3% share followed by CustoSolution at 24.8%, CostAlert at 16.7%, and all others accounting for 22.2% market share. The industry structure is in win/lose and is moving from early maturity to late maturity.

Figure 4.1 StructureScape

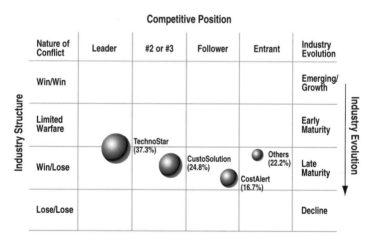

To build a StructureScape for your market, plot your group and the competitors using a relative measure of the market (revenue, market share, sales volume, etc.) based on the following three parameters:

1. Market Position
   a. Leader
   b. Company Number 2 or 3
   c. Follower
   d. New Entrant
2. Industry Evolution
   a. Emerging
   b. Early Maturity
   c. Late Maturity
   d. Decline
3. Nature of Conflict
   a. Win/Win
   b. Limited Warfare
   c. Win/Lose
   d. Lose/Lose

Five Forces of Competition

Introduced by Harvard Business School Professor Michael Porter, this model assesses the environment and industry structure based on the five factors that have the most significant impact on the business's profitability.[7] In completing the model, it is helpful to rate each of the five factors as either "Low," "Medium," or "High," and record relevant comments next to each.

1. Barriers to Entry
   - Economies of scale
   - Product differentiation
   - Brand equity
   - Switching costs
   - Capital requirements
   - Intellectual capital

2. Power of Buyers
   - Number of key customers
   - Number of alternative sources
   - Customers' switching costs
   - Customers' profitability
   - Threat of forward or backward integration

3. Substitutes
   - Availability of close substitutes
   - User's switching costs
   - Substitute price-value

4. Power of Suppliers
   - Number of key suppliers
   - Number of substitutes for supplier's products
   - Suppliers contribution to quality/service
   - Threat of forward or backward integration

5. Industry Competition
   - Concentration of competitors
   - Industry growth
   - Product differentiation
   - Strategic stakes

Figure 4.2 illustrates the Five Forces of Competition Analysis for the medical device arena in which TechnoStar, CostAlert, and CustoSolution play.

We note from the example the following market insights:

- Threat of new entrants is medium due to the proprietary technology requirements;
- The bargaining power of buyers is high because of growing pricing transparency;

Figure 4.2 Five Forces of Competition

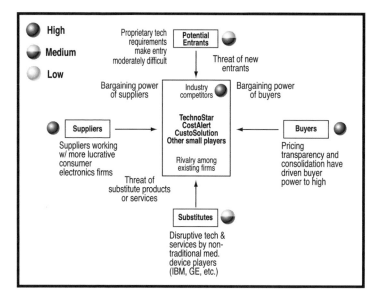

- The threat of substitute products is medium, and non-traditional players with disruptive technologies need to be monitored;

- The bargaining power of suppliers is high because they are also working with consumer electronics firms that offer substantially higher revenue than the medical device companies;

- Industry competition is high among the three primary players and smaller secondary players.

CUSTOMERS

The terms "customer-centric," "customer-focused," and "customer-oriented" can be heard in the hallways and conference rooms of nearly every company. The challenge is to back those words up with meaningful action that delivers on those promises. Meaningful action starts with intimate knowledge of customers and their value drivers.

The following three models are helpful in achieving a deeper understanding of customers in order to craft strategy that provides them with superior value:

1. Customer Matrix
2. Service Map
3. Value Driver Matrix

Customer Matrix

The Customer Matrix provides a comprehensive look at the base of customers and their influence on the decision to purchase or not purchase your offerings. To construct a Customer Matrix, list the market segments or customer groups across the top of the chart. Place the customer segments along the left side of the matrix and the target audiences in the cells of the matrix. Finally, rate each target audience member's role as a Decision Maker (D), Influencer (I), or Implementer (M) to gauge their contribution.

The Customer Matrix in Figure 4.3 depicts the potential decision makers in a hospital system for our three medical device companies. The market segments for the hospital system run across the top of the chart and the customer segments along the left side. Within the matrix, the specific customer targets are identified and then categorized based on their role in the decision-making process. (Note the following designations: RN—Registered Nurse; RPh—Registered Pharmacist).

Figure 4.3 Customer Matrix

	Group Purchasing Organization	Integrated Delivery Networks	Hospitals	Regulatory Agencies
Clinical	RN Specialities RPh Specialities	Med. Dir. RN Specialities RPh Specialities	RN Mgr. RN Educ. Dir. RPh	RN w/MBA RPh w/MBA
Financial	RN w/MBA Material Mgr.	RN w/MBA Material Mgr.	Material Mgr.	N/A
Biomed.	Biomed.	Biomed.	Dir. Biomed.	Former Dir. Biomed.
IT	IT Exec.	IT Exec.	Dir. IT	Informatics PhD
Legal/Risk	Contract Lawyer	Contract Lawyer	Risk Mgr.	Clinical Background
C-Suite	CEO, CFO, CIO, CMO, COO	CEO, CFO, CIO, CMO, COO	CEO, CFO, CIO, CMO, COO, CNO	President

Decision Maker ■ Implementer ☐ Influencer & Implementer ☐ Influencer ☐

Service Map

A study by the Forum Corporation reports that customers are five times more likely to switch to a competitor because of poor service than because of poor product quality or price issues.[8] Research has also shown that customers are willing to pay up to 30% more for an average product if they receive outstanding service from the company.[9] A Service Map can reduce those customer defections and increase the value of your offerings.

The Service Map is a visual aid for picturing the inputs, activities, outputs, people, and resources involved in satisfying a customer's need for your product or service. It acts as a tangible blueprint to assess exactly how efficient or inefficient the customer is being served. Relative to strategy development, the Service Map gives you a quantifiable way to determine where and in what amount current resources are being allocated. Once you know exactly how your current resources are being used, you can optimally allocate resources in the future. The ability to measure the different facets of your service process (i.e., time it takes the legal department to approve a contract) is of great value in identifying areas of excellence and areas in need of improvement.

A Service Map for the medical device example is depicted in Figure 4.4 with all of the activities above the midline "visible to customer" and all the activities below the midline "invisible to customer." The service process moves from left to right, initiated in the lower left-hand corner with "marketing providing a target client list" to sales reps and concluding in the lower right-hand corner with the "sales rep contacting operations to begin work."

Once the "as is" map is created and reviewed, a "should be" map can be constructed and used to measure the process moving forward. Measurements can include the time it takes to move from one step to the next, the time an individual or department holds the process at their point, and the effectiveness of each of the individual components (i.e., sales closing rates, contracts won, etc.).

Designing your Service Map entails the following seven steps:
1. Define the service process.
   - Set the process boundaries.
   - Identify the goals of the service process map.
   - Prepare a one-page brief outlining the deliverables, accountability, and time frame.

Figure 4.4 Service Map

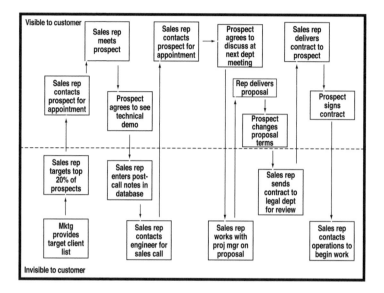

2. Generate a list of issues to be addressed.
   - Current performance gaps between company and customer expectations.
   - Current performance gaps between company and competitors.

3. Complete a Process Profile Worksheet.
   - One-page template that captures the critical process information:

a. Process champion	e. Triggers
b. Process description	f. Inputs
c. Customer value drivers	g. Activities
d. Customer value driver metrics	h. Outputs

4. Create the "as is" service process map.
   - Visually depict the service process as it is currently being performed, including people, resources, actions, forms, reports, metrics, etc.

5. Review the "as is" service process map.
   - Determine effectiveness and efficiency of current process.
   - Identify bottlenecks, non-value adds, structural, and resource issues.
   - Create a list of best practices for each step.

6. Create the "should be" map.
   - Use basic flowchart symbols to create the map.
   - Create a list of potential obstacles in launching the new map and ways to overcome them.

7. Implement the "should be" map.
   - Pilot test the "should be" map.
   - Train employees on the new map.
   - Develop a feedback mechanism.
   - Benchmark revised metrics.

Value Driver Matrix

Determining what is of the greatest value to customers and then shaping your offering to deliver on that value is an important element in good business planning. The Value Driver Matrix provides a means of aligning customer groups and value drivers to understand what level of importance each factor has to customers. Clearly demarcating the level of value the factors have with the different customer groups allows you to more effectively allocate resources to those areas that will have the most impact.

We can see in Figure 4.5 the customer targets for the hospital along the left side and the potential value drivers across the top of the chart, and spheres indicating whether the factor is of low, medium, or high value to that particular customer group.

Figure 4.5 Value Driver Matrix

High ● / Medium ◗ / Low ○	Ease-of-Use	Efficacy	Safety	Product training	Consulting service	Price	Clinical education
Clinical	●	●	●	●	◗	◗	●
Financial	○	●	○	●	○	●	○
Biomedical	●	●	●	●	○	○	○
IT	●	●	●	●	◗	○	○
Legal/risk	○	●	●	○	●	○	◗
C-Suite	○	●	○	●	○	◗	◗

To create a Value Driver Matrix, list the customers on the left side of the chart and list the potential value drivers across the top of the chart. Using the symbols for low, medium, and high, rate the level of value on each factor for each of the customer groups. This will allow for more effective and efficient targeting of resources in product design, marketing, and communication vehicles.

COMPETITORS

The goal of business strategy is to outperform competitors. However, it's not uncommon to see companies working at one of two extremes—in a vacuum with little awareness of what the competition is doing, or obsessing with competitors to the point that all of their activities are simply reactions to competitor moves. Strategic thinking helps us inhabit that interactive middle ground that provides us with constant awareness of a competitor's key activities and a direction-resilient drive toward our goals.

The following three models serve as a useful guide to mapping the competitive landscape and provide insight into gaining and maintaining competitive advantage:

1. Strategy Profile
2. Spider Map
3. Competitive Advantage

Strategy Profile

The Strategy Profile is a valuable tool for visualizing strategy on the competitive landscape. It does so by comparing investment levels in resource allocation according to the key areas of industry competition. The Strategy Profile provides insight into three areas:

1) It maps the industry landscape by presenting the factors that determine competitive position.

2) It captures the individual strategy profiles of the market players.

3) It creates the company's strategy profile, identifying where and to what degree it invests its resources.[10]

Using the Strategy Profile to understand where you and your competitors are investing their resources, and to what level, is an effective means of determining where your true differentiation exists.

To construct a Strategy Profile for your business, complete the following steps:

1. List the areas of potential investment in the left column.

2. List the key competitors across the top row.

3. Rate the players for each factor on a scale of 1 - 10, with 1 being a low investment and 10 being a high investment.

For the medical device arena, we list the three competitors across the top and the areas of investment along the left side. We then rate each of their levels of investment for the respective factors using the 1 – 10 scale (Figure 4.6).

Figure 4.6 Strategy Profile—Step 1

	TechnoStar	CostAlert	CustoSolution
R&D	10	1	3
Sales Force	5	3	8
Consulting	1	1	9
Education	8	2	2
Marketing	9	5	3
Alliances	2	2	6
Service	4	2	8

Next, place the areas of investment along the X-axis. Then, plot the scores for each area using different lines/colors for your offerings, and those of relevant competitors, and label them accordingly.

Figure 4.7 Strategy Profile—Step 2

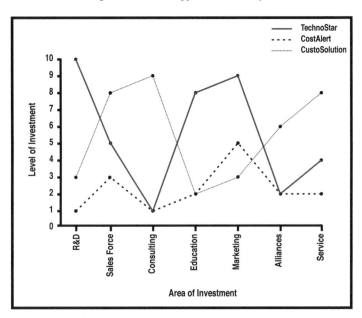

Figure 4.7 shows the strategy curves for the three competitors. We can see that TechnoStar invests significantly more in R&D, education, and marketing than its competitors; CustoSolution places their biggest investments in service, consulting, and its sales force; and CostAlert has a minimum investment across the board, which allows them to maintain lower costs and charge lower prices.

Spider Map

A Spider Map enables you to visually capture the gaps between the attributes of your offerings and the attributes of your competitor's offerings to assess where differentiation exists. A common question is "What's the difference between the Strategy Profile and the Spider Map?" The Strategy Profile depicts the differences between competitors based on *resource allocation* such as sales force, R&D, training and education, etc. It compares how competitors are investing their limited capital, talent, and time. The Spider Map shows the differences between competitors based on the *attributes* (characteristics) of the competitor's offerings—things such as product performance, speed, efficacy, safety, etc.

In evaluating the attributes of the three competitors, Figure 4.8 shows TechnoStar's offering has the best ease-of-use, efficacy, adverse event profile, and design. CostAlert provides custom-

Figure 4.8 Spider Map

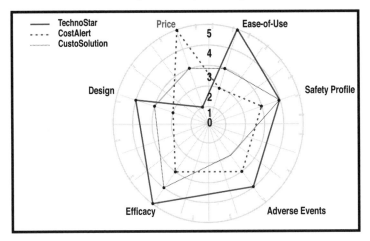

ers with the lowest cost; and CustoSolution finds itself in "no man's land" from a product attribute standpoint, as it has invested in the service aspect (consulting) of the business.

The Spider Map is developed by completing the following steps:

1. Identify the key attributes (usually between four and eight) for entrants in the market and label the Spider Map with them.
2. Rate each competitor's offering for the attributes using a scale of 1 – 5, with 1 being low and 5 being high.
3. Plot each competitor's scores for the respective attributes and connect the points to form each entrant's attribute web.
4. Assess the map to determine the positive and negative attribute gaps and utilize the information in developing future strategy.

Competitive Advantage

Earlier we described strategy as performing different activities than competitors or performing similar activities in a different manner.[11] Just as the essence of strategy involves intelligently allocating resources (time, talent, and money) through a unique system of activities, the activities make up the basic units of competitive advantage. So, to understand competitive advantage or lack thereof, we need to assess the activity system.

The capabilities (or more popularly, "core competencies") allow us to perform activities, which in turn enable our offerings to the market. Visually, the schematic is as follows:

Capabilities

Activities

Offerings

Capabilities are made up of assets and core competencies, and are classified as one of two types: distinctive or reproducible. Distinctive capabilities are those that cannot be emulated by competitors, or can only be emulated with extreme difficulty. Reproducible capabilities are those that can be successfully replicated by competitors.

Activities are the means for channeling capabilities (resources) in order to create offerings for the marketplace. We say activities are the basic units of competitive advantage because they are where capabilities merge with resource allocation to transform into the things that impact customers. The activities you choose to invest in—or just as important, not invest in—determine your strategic focus.

The weapons we ultimately brandish in our competitive battles come in the form of offerings. Offerings are the manifestation of the group's efforts in terms of products and/or services.

The emergence of competitive advantage then comes through three steps:

1. Customers perceive a consistent difference between offerings and that difference occurs in an attribute that impacts the buying decision.

2. The difference in the offering stems from a distinctive capability.

3. Both the offering difference and the distinctive capability last over time.[12]

To objectively determine competitive advantage, we use the chart in Figure 4.9 to assess the three components and compare the three competitors.

Figure 4.9 Competitive Advantage Assessment

	TechnoStar	CostAlert	CustoSolution
Capabilities	- Premier R&D personnel - Marketing infrastructure & personnel	- Operational effectiveness model - Virtual company model	- Consulting personnel - Clinical & business training
Activities	- Thought-leader support - Marketing department shaping industry treatment guidelines	- Outsourced manufacturing & production - Sales-driven processes	- Physician referral program - Customer Advisory Board
Offerings	- Premier technology	- Most cost-effective technology	- Customized technology solutions

As you move forward in the strategy development process, consider the four general methods for influencing competitive advantage:

1. Change the offerings (i.e., Whirlpool).
2. Create new capabilities (i.e., Apple's iPod).
3. Shape customer's value preferences (i.e., Oreck).
4. Change the dimensions of competition (i.e., Cirque de Soleil). [13]

Ask yourself, what can our group do to maintain or alter competitive advantage in the market?

COMPANY

It is difficult to look in the mirror and objectively identify our strengths and weaknesses. That's one of the reasons why using an external resource as the strategy development team leader is recommended. Management guru Peter Drucker uses the following analogy:

Physicians learned long ago not to treat their own families, let alone themselves. The professional needs commitment to the client's cause or to the patient's recovery. But he must stay free of involvement. He must not himself be a part of the situation. And the practicing executive is always a part of the situation... The executive in an organization is also always a member of the organization, shares its traditions, its beliefs, its joys and its sorrows, its greatness and its pettiness. He is like the physician who treats his own family—he diagnoses with the heart and always takes his own pulse rather than that of the patient.[14]

Making the most of a company's resources begins with a thorough assessment of those resources to determine what is driving the success and what has simply been along for the ride. The following three models provide a start to generating insights about the company:

1. SWOT Analysis
2. Opportunity & Threat Matrices
3. Activity System Map

SWOT Analysis

Like most things utterly familiar, the SWOT analysis has been taken for granted to the point that it has become the most mis-used tool in the manager's box. A good SWOT analysis is one of the cornerstones of good strategy. A half-baked SWOT analysis (and most of them are) prevents businesses from real-izing their full potential and marries them to mediocrity. Let's look at what it takes to move from doing a SWOT analysis nearly right to doing it exactly right—a difference which can jumpstart your strategy.

The SWOT Analysis provides a simple yet comprehensive method for examining the strategic fit between a firm's in-ternal capabilities (strengths and weaknesses) and external possibilities (opportunities and threats).

The acronym SWOT stands for:

- Strengths
- Weaknesses
- Opportunities
- Threats

Strengths are those factors that make a group more competi-tive than its peers. Strengths are tasks that the group has a distinctive advantage at accomplishing, or superior resources and capabilities that the group holds that can be effectively used to achieve its performance objectives.

Weaknesses are limitations, faults, or defects within the group that will keep it from achieving its objectives. A weakness is what a group does poorly and where it has inferior capabilities or resources as compared to its peers.

Opportunities include any favorable current or prospective situation in the group's environment such as a trend, change, or overlooked need that supports the demand for a product or service and permits the group to enhance its competitive position.

A threat includes any unfavorable situation, trend, or impending change in a group's environment that is currently or potentially damaging or threatening to its ability to compete. It may be a barrier, constraint, or anything that might inflict problems, damage, harm, or injury to the group.

In general, strengths and weaknesses (internal environment) are made up of factors over which the group has greater relative control. These factors may include the following:

- Resources (people, money, time)
- Skill sets
- Knowledge base
- Processes and systems, including operational and customer-facing
- Staffing practices
- Brand
- Values
- Culture

Opportunities and threats (external environment) are made up of those factors over which the organization has influence but not control. These factors include:

- Overall demand
- Competitor activity

- Market saturation
- Government policies
- Economic conditions
- Social, cultural, and ethical developments
- Technological developments

The SWOT analysis model helps us answer two fundamental questions:

1. What do we have (strengths and weaknesses)?
2. What might we do (opportunities and threats)?

Five SWOT Killers

As with any model, the reason a SWOT analysis is performed is to generate insights about the business and drive planning efforts. There are five SWOT killers that we need to be aware of to prevent our efforts from being an exercise in futility:

1. The Laundry List

When listing the individual elements under each category, give careful thought to the importance of each item. A laundry list of seven to ten factors for each category is fine in the first draft. However, only the elements with significant impact on the business should be recorded in the final analysis (approximately three to five). Marshaling the mental discipline to create a tight SWOT analysis enables you to move into planning mode with greater clarity and focus—two keys to strong strategy.

2. Generalities

There is a fine line between the factors in the SWOT analysis being brief and being meaningless. How many times have you seen a SWOT analysis with "quality" listed under the strengths or weaknesses column? That's about as useful as putting down the word "the." The factors listed need to be specific enough so that someone reading the analysis without the creator sitting next to them can understand, to a reasonable degree, what is meant by the factor. Recording "manufacturing line breakdowns" rather than "quality" as a weakness is much more helpful because it alerts the reader to the specific cause of the issue.

3. Cause and Effects

Another common mistake is listing the effect rather than the cause of a strength or weakness. An example of a strength often listed is "#1 market share." It's much more helpful to list the cause of that number one market share—i.e., consultative selling skills of sales reps, 3:1 advertising spend ratio versus the competition, etc. Listing the cause also plays another important role by allowing managers to more easily identify and share best practices among the group. Knowing what's driving market share leadership can be usefully applied to other groups within the organization.

4. Mistaking Influence for Control

Despite the clearly defined lines of strengths/weaknesses being internal and controllable and opportunities/threats being external and influenced, factors are often mistakenly placed in the model. The rule of thumb is if you can allocate your resources to a factor and control it, it is a strength/weakness. If your resource allocation can influence but not necessarily control the factor, it is an opportunity/threat.

5. Not Quantifying Opportunities & Threats

Think way back to those lectures on Einstein's theories of general and special relativity (as painful as that might be). In modern physics, the mass of an object is a relative quantity. In the world of SWOT analysis, the size of opportunities and threats are relative quantities as well. Managers of two different brands both might list the opportunity of "large Medicare population" for their medical device product. However, "large" for one manager might mean a $2 million opportunity while "large" for the other manager might mean a $20 million opportunity. If the opportunity is not quantified in the SWOT analysis, the decision as to where to allocate resources becomes hazier and much more vulnerable to error. Quantifying opportunities and threats allows you to more confidently allocate your limited resources to those that will provide the greatest return on investment.

Sometimes we don't have all of the necessary data to make an exact quantification of the opportunity/threat. That's when expertise comes into play, so move forward and give a rough percentage or ratio (i.e., competitor ad spending is greater than 2:1 in this market segment). Figure 4.10 represents the SWOT Analysis for CustoSolution.

Opportunity and Threat Matrices

Opportunity and Threat Matrices provide us with the vehicles to do a deep dive in the areas of promise and challenge for the business. They are an objective means of prioritizing opportunities and threats based on two important criteria: probability and impact.

The Opportunity Matrix examines opportunities based on their probability of achievement and impact on our business if they are achieved. The Threat Matrix, originally presented by marketer Terry Richey, assesses threats on their probability of occurrence and impact on our business if they do occur.[15] The matrices are a natural evolution of the SWOT Analysis and function as barometers that dictate the areas and levels of future resource allocation.

The matrices are created by plotting the opportunities and threats generated in the SWOT Analysis according to their

Figure 4.10 SWOT Analysis—CustoSolution

Strengths	Weaknesses
1. Customer knowledge due to consulting services 2. Established base of contracts 3. Breadth of product portfolio	1. Non-competitive marketing resources (outspent 3:1) 2. Siloed approach to growth 3. R&D investment level (outspent 5:1) 4. Timely resolution to customer quality issues (60 days)
Opportunities	Threats
1. Outpatient facilities product use (25% of mkt) 2. Baby boomer segment (2/3 of patients) 3. Expansion of consulting services (75% of current product customers not using)	1. Competitor alliances with non-traditional players 2. Increasing power of buyers (consolidation) 3. Customers awarding non-exclusive agreements (35%)

ratings on two scales: probability and impact. For both probability and impact, we use scales of 1 (low) to 10 (high). Resource allocation can then be influenced by where the opportunities/threats fall. Those plotted in Level 1 will receive the most resources, those in Level 2 less resources and those in Level 3 may only receive monitoring.

From the CustoSolution SWOT Analysis, we take the opportunities identified and plot them on the Opportunity Matrix shown in Figure 4.11.

Figure 4.11 Opportunity Matrix

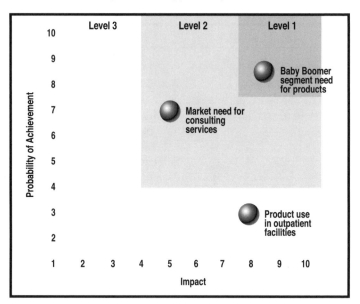

We then take the threats identified for CustoSolution and plot them on the Threat Matrix as in Figure 4.12.

Activity System Map

The Activity System Map is a visual representation of your organization's strategy and the tactics that support it. It provides a 30,000 foot view of the business by capturing the strategy, tactics, and relationships between the two on a single page. Building an Activity System Map first requires the individual to step back and view their business from the high ground to better understand the strategic composition. It then drills down to assemble a conceptual framework, identifying the

Figure 4.12 Threat Matrix

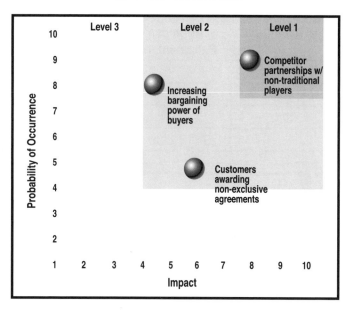

interrelationships and competencies of the key facets of the business. Once completed, the Activity System Map provides a clear and concise picture of the business that enables leaders to more effectively set direction and make resource allocation decisions.

While a strategy can be made up of only one activity, there are compelling reasons for building an activity system to drive your strategy. As discussed in Chapter One, when the number of activities comprising your strategy increases, it becomes more and more difficult for competitors to emulate your entire system of strategy (Figure 4.13).

Figure 4.13 Arithmetic for System of Activities

# of Activities	Numerical Representation	Probability of competitor match
1	.9	90%
2	.9 x .9	81%
3	.9 x .9 x .9	73%
4	.9 x .9 x .9 x .9	66%
10	$.9^{10}$	35%

The Activity System Map is comprised of large spheres which represent the strategic themes of the organization, and small spheres which represent individual activities or tactics. Most groups have between three and five strategic themes driving their business.

In addition to identifying the individual strategic themes and tactics, the Activity System Map serves to highlight the strength of the relationships between the strategy and tactics. A solid line between two spheres indicates direct support and a dotted line indicates indirect support.

The Activity System Map for CustoSolution is demonstrated in Figure 4.14. The three strategic themes for CustoSolution are customer intimacy, customized services, and grass roots marketing, all represented by large spheres. The activities and tactics supporting each of those strategic themes are shown as the smaller spheres attached with a solid (direct support) or dotted (indirect support) line.

Figure 4.14 Activity System Map

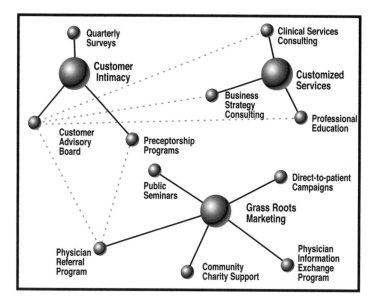

Following are the steps to designing an Activity System Map for your group:

1. Identify and plot the three to five strategic themes.

2. Attach the tactics that are currently being employed.

3. Add tactics that would strengthen strategic themes.

4. Rate the tactics around each strategic theme relative to one another on their level of impact (Low—Medium—High).

5. Consider eliminating tactics with "low" impact.

After creating the Activity System Map, ask the following checking questions:

1. Do the strategic themes collectively embody a differentiated strategy from the competition?
2. Is each tactic supporting at least one strategic theme?
3. What is the overall level of tactical value (connectivity + impact)?
4. Is each tactic directly or indirectly relevant to customers?
5. Sketch a key competitor's Activity System Map. What insights can you draw from comparing your Activity System Map with that of the competitor's?

Strategic Thinking Wrap-up

We reviewed twelve models that are effective in facilitating the strategic thinking process and there are numerous others that you can use to add to the group's portfolio for future sessions. After the group completes the appropriate models in the four areas of market, customers, competitors, and company, it's important to capture the output in its visual format and provide it to the team members individually. This will allow them to continue to think through the key issues and provides an incubation period for additional insights.

Using a methodical and comprehensive modeling process to facilitate group strategic thinking provides a significant indirect benefit. Once the group has been through the process and properly instructed on how to use the models, they can use them on a regular basis to think through their respective businesses. In essence, the process provides a high-level training experience on the strategy development process which enables managers to become more effective strategists.

DIFFERENCE MAKERS

- The strategic thinking phase is crucial because it offers the opportunity to challenge assumptions, spark innovation, and catalyze the insights that will drive future success.

- Strategic thinking is the generation of business insights. Strategic planning then channels those insights into an action plan to most effectively allocate resources to meet the company's goals and objectives.

- Strategic thinking is not limited to a phase in the strategy development process; rather, it is a skill set that the entire organization should be working to develop and practice on a daily basis.

- World-class organizations such as GE are developing training and tools for their managers to become more effective strategists.

- Modeling is the platform on which the strategic thinking phase is built. Models provide a visual method of extracting the group's insights and capturing those insights in a tangible medium.

- The strategic thinking phase is categorized into the four key areas of any business: market, customers, competitors, and company. Methodically moving through these four areas and utilizing the appropriate models within each ensures a comprehensive and meaningful examination of the business.

- For each section of the strategic thinking phase, three sample models are presented:

Continued on next page

- ○ Market

    1. PEST Analysis—A review of the political, economic, social, and technological factors influencing the business.

    2. StructureScape—A method for plotting the size/influence of each of the market players relative to the market leader using market share, size, sales volume, etc.

    3. Five Forces of Competition—An assessment of the environment and industry structure based on the five factors that have the most significant impact on a business's profitability.

- ○ Customers

    1. Customer Matrix—A comprehensive look at the base of customers and their influence on the decision to purchase or not purchase your offerings.

    2. Service Map—A visual aid for picturing the inputs, activities, outputs, people, and resources involved in satisfying a customer's need for your product or service. It acts as a tangible blueprint to assess exactly how efficient or inefficient the customer is being served.

    3. Value Driver Matrix—A tool that provides a means of aligning customer groups and their value drivers to understand what level of importance each factor has to customers.

- ○ Competitors

    1. Strategy Profile—A valuable tool for visualizing strategy on the competitive landscape by com-

Continued on next page

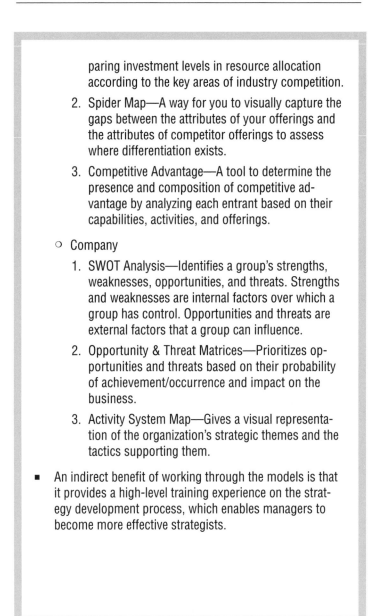

paring investment levels in resource allocation according to the key areas of industry competition.

2. Spider Map—A way for you to visually capture the gaps between the attributes of your offerings and the attributes of competitor offerings to assess where differentiation exists.

3. Competitive Advantage—A tool to determine the presence and composition of competitive advantage by analyzing each entrant based on their capabilities, activities, and offerings.

○ Company

1. SWOT Analysis—Identifies a group's strengths, weaknesses, opportunities, and threats. Strengths and weaknesses are internal factors over which a group has control. Opportunities and threats are external factors that a group can influence.

2. Opportunity & Threat Matrices—Prioritizes opportunities and threats based on their probability of achievement/occurrence and impact on the business.

3. Activity System Map—Gives a visual representation of the organization's strategic themes and the tactics supporting them.

■ An indirect benefit of working through the models is that it provides a high-level training experience on the strategy development process, which enables managers to become more effective strategists.

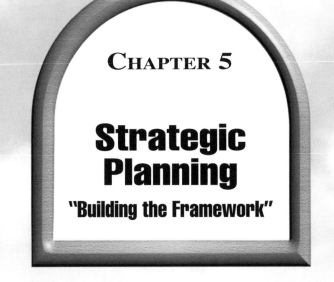

CHAPTER 5

Strategic Planning
"Building the Framework"

*All parts of the system must be constructed
with reference to all other parts, since, in one
sense, all the parts form one whole.*

– Thomas Edison
Inventor

The true mastery of the sculptor emerges as she synthesizes her vision of the art into a skeletal structure that serves as the work's foundation. This synthesis requires the mental dexterity to marry images, materials, and tools in just the right proportion to create the finished product.

Using a proven strategy development process provides a framework in which to house all the complex, intertwining elements of a business. It ensures that you've considered each of the key elements and enables you to begin piecing them together to develop a winning strategy. In essence, the strategic planning phase involves channeling the insights and intelligence generated from the discovery and strategic thinking phases into an action plan to achieve goals and objectives.

Once the group has worked through the designated models in the strategic thinking phase, there are several key issues to be addressed prior to setting the goals, objectives, strategies, and tactics. Those issues include the following items:

- **Business Model Analysis**—a concise method of determining the context, who, what, how, and strategy shield that comprise the building blocks of a business.

- **Purpose**—mission, vision, and values.

- **Value Discipline**—the decision to focus on one of the following three disciplines: 1) operational excellence, 2) product leadership, or 3) customer intimacy.

- **Value Proposition**—a clearly articulated statement of the value you deliver to customers.

- **Position**—the place you want your offering to own in the customer's mind.

- **SWOT Alignment**—a matrix designed to combine the internal capabilities (strengths and weaknesses) with the external possibilities (opportunities and threats) to begin crafting potential strategies.

- **Growth Strategies**—thoughtful selection of a combination of the five growth strategies to create a portfolio of initiatives to grow the business.

- **Strategy Formula**—a tool for articulating strategy in a clear, effective, and consistent manner.

- **StrategyPrint**—a two-page business blueprint that serves as a visual executive summary and provides the all-important link between strategic planning and daily activity.

Business Model Analysis

The business model analysis identifies the building blocks on which the business exists. While they are often taken for granted, the business model elements provide the framework for a thoughtful kick-off discussion on the fundamentals of the business. There are five key pieces to consider when assessing the business model:

Context: The combination of market opportunities and core competencies that have allowed the business to enter and exist within the industry.

Who: The targeted customers that use the products/services and their value drivers.

What: The specific offerings provided to customers.

How: The capabilities that provide a unique offering to customers.

Strategy Shield: The barriers in place to prevent competitors from taking business.

Figure 5.0 provides a look at the business models of the three competitors. As we might expect, TechnoStar's investments in innovation have provided it with a strong strategy shield in advanced proprietary technology. Meanwhile, CostAlert's focus on operational excellence has allowed it to provide low-cost offerings that carry with them the risk of no strategy shield.

Figure 5.0 Business Model Analysis

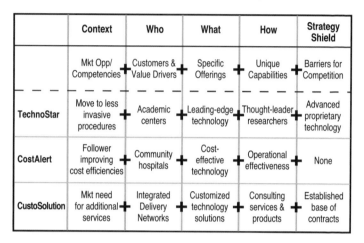

	Context	Who	What	How	Strategy Shield
	Mkt Opp/ Competencies +	Customers & Value Drivers +	Specific Offerings +	Unique Capabilities +	Barriers for Competition
TechnoStar	Move to less invasive procedures +	Academic centers +	Leading-edge technology +	Thought-leader researchers +	Advanced proprietary technology
CostAlert	Follower improving cost efficiencies +	Community hospitals +	Cost-effective technology +	Operational effectiveness +	None
CustoSolution	Mkt need for additional + services	Integrated Delivery Networks +	Customized technology solutions +	Consulting services & products +	Established base of contracts

Purpose

A group's purpose can be represented in three ways as shown in Figure 5.1:

Figure 5.1 Organization's Purpose

A mission is a clear, concise, and enduring statement of the reasons for an organization's existence today. A vision represents future purpose, providing a mental picture of the aspirational existence that an organization is working toward. Supporting both the current and future purpose are values. Values are the ideals and principles that guide the thoughts and actions of an organization and define its character. Working together, mission, vision, and values provide a powerful directional force for unifying and coordinating actions and decisions to ensure the optimal use of resources.

As strategy is concerned with the intelligent allocation of limited resources, we can see that identifying a current and future purpose is critical. From a strategic thinking perspective, establishing a clear and compelling purpose provides the general basis or criteria on which resource allocation decisions should be made and measured against. Without purpose, the rationale for decision making becomes subjective and disconnected from the goals and objectives trying to be achieved. For the detailed process on how to create mission, vision and values statements, please reference my book *Storm Rider: Becoming a Strategic Thinker*.

Value Discipline

Research by Michael Treacy and Fred Wiersema of more than 80 market leading companies demonstrated that successful companies can be categorized by one of three distinct value disciplines:[1]

1. Operational Excellence
2. Product Leadership
3. Customer Intimacy

The research showed that successful companies choose one of the three value disciplines to excel in and maintain industry-average thresholds in the other two. From a strategy perspective, that means that the majority of a firm's discretionary resources are allocated toward only one of the three areas. This principle flies in the face of the human disposition toward balance and equilibrium. Good strategy requires the trade-offs to load resources into one area and put only a minimal amount in the other two value disciplines.

Operational Excellence

Companies focusing on the operational excellence value discipline are characterized as having the best total cost as exemplified earlier by our fictitious medical device company CostAlert. They provide customers with reliable offerings at competitive prices and deliver those offerings in an efficient manner. Examples of companies that have chosen to dedicate their resources to the operational excellence value discipline include Wal-Mart, Dell, Southwest Airlines, McDonalds, and FedEx to name a few. These companies realize that standardization and efficiency are the lifeblood of their businesses.

Product Leadership

As one would guess, product leadership is all about providing the best product—one that offers true differentiation in the marketplace. Successful product leaders produce products and services that customers recognize as being the best—offerings that add significant benefits and performance to customers. The fictitious medical device company TechnoStar played this role in the earlier modeling examples.

Product leaders' primary source of competition is themselves—working fast and furiously to make their older offerings obsolete with new state-of-the-art products. Examples of product leadership companies include Nike, 3M, Apple, and Lexus. They understand that they provide premium brands, and more important, they build value propositions that enable them to get paid premium prices for their brands. From a strategy perspective, the majority of their resources are allocated to their people and R&D efforts—the two primary sources of continued product superiority and innovation.

Customer Intimacy

Customer-intimate firms offer the best total solution to customers as demonstrated in the earlier modeling exercises by CustoSolution. They live on the depth and length of relationships to their customers—relationships that are built on understanding exactly what customers need and how to deliver it in a tailored fashion. These companies include IBM, GE, and Nordstrom's.

Not selecting and emphasizing a single value discipline results in three undesirable effects:

1. Fractured Strategic Direction
2. Weakened Brand
3. Mediocrity & Commoditization

Fractured Strategic Direction

A fractured strategic direction occurs when an organization lacks the discipline to focus the majority of its resources in just one of the three areas of value. Usually, in a well-meaning but ill-conceived attempt to grow the business, their resources begin migrating to several of the value disciplines. This resource migration serves to muddy the strategic direction and compromise growth in the long term. As we saw in the examples provided for each of the three disciplines, the truly successful companies are clearly committed to excelling in only one of the three disciplines, while maintaining parity in the other two.

Weakened Brand

Aligning your group around a focus on one of the three value disciplines is a critical component of robust strategy. One of the primary challenges to alignment around a value discipline is ensuring that all of the different functional areas are "singing from the same song sheet." This analogy is especially appropriate because not having internal groups aligned around the same value discipline is manifested in their communications to customers. It's quite common (but dead wrong) for the marketing and R&D teams to be working and promoting from the product leadership value discipline while the sales force is selling on price. This internal conflict has real-world external effects because it blurs the value of the offering to customers and creates false expectations.

Mediocrity & Commoditization

Allocating resources evenly between the three value disciplines is the most insidious cause of business failure. It is not marked by heated debate between functional groups or diametrically opposed initiatives. It simply prevents a company from realizing its true potential and condemns it to the slow and steady damnation of surviving instead of thriving.

Intertwining Strategy & Value

Once the group has determined which of the three value disciplines to emphasize, the process of value engineering needs to take place. Value engineering encompasses the reallocation of investments according to the value discipline that is being used to drive success. This reallocation requires a baseline assessment of how resources are currently being allocated and in which areas they should be shifted. This step will likely meet with some internal resistance because it requires that dreaded six-letter word: change.

As resource allocation is at the heart of strategy, it's important to make sure that everyone in the group understands the strategy and why resources are being focused in one value discipline. A powerful tool in communicating this manifestation of strategy is the value proposition.

Value Proposition

Building on the value discipline, the value proposition is a succinct statement describing the offering—the bundle of products and services, their attributes and position, customer experience, and benefits. Correctly done, the value proposition serves as a beacon both internally and externally to convey the essence of the group's work. It provides a compass for employees to guide everyone's work toward the same ends. The value proposition also ensures that a unified message is being delivered to customers from all of the different customer touch points in the organization.

There are seven steps in the process of developing a value proposition:

1. Identify the major attributes customers value through primary or secondary research.
2. Weigh the importance of the different attributes.
3. Assess the company's and competitor's performances (ability to deliver) on the weighted customer values.
4. Further examine how customers in different segments rate the importance of the attribute and the company's performance relative to the competition.

5. Based on the analysis, write the value proposition accordingly.

6. Evaluate the proposed value proposition statement with the following criteria:
   - Relevance to customers
   - Group's ability to deliver
   - Differentiation from the competition
   - Delivery on key metrics

7. Continuously monitor customer values over time to detect shifts and make modifications.

As an example, the value propositions of TechnoStar, CostAlert, and CustoSolution can be seen in the following statements:

TechnoStar—"Designing superior products that provide state-of-the-art care."

CostAlert—"Delivering reliable products that offer the most cost-effective care."

CustoSolution—"Tailoring a system of products to seamlessly fit with your needs."

Position

Focus is achieved through making trade-offs and using those trade-offs to allocate resources to support a singular position. A position is defined as the place you own in the customer's mind. Examples of positions:

➢ Volvo .... Safety
➢ Rolex .... Status
➢ Krispy Kreme .... Mouth-watering taste
➢ Wal-Mart .... Low prices

There are five phases in the position development process (Figure 5.2):

Figure 5.2 Position Development Process

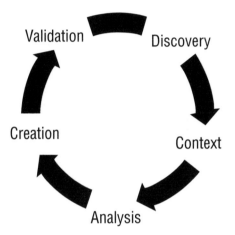

1. The discovery phase involves compiling all relevant business information, including primary research (employee and customer interviews) and secondary data sources relevant to the position.

2. The context phase involves a deep dive into the position by a core positioning team. Disciplined and comprehensive strategic thinking is channeled into the four areas: market, customers, competitors, and the organization. The result is a challenging of business assumptions and the generation of new insights relative to how the firm is positioned.

3. The analysis phase allows for a thorough review of all information, intelligence, and insights about the position and answers the question: "So what?—What do these insights mean relative to positioning?"

4. The creation phase involves building the positioning platform and writing positioning statements to capture the essence of the new position.

5. The validation phase includes evaluating the recommended position on five criteria:
   ➤ Credible—Is the position believable?
   ➤ Ownable—Is the position unique in the market?
   ➤ Relevant—Is the position important to customers?
   ➤ Defensible—Can the position be supported with data and initiatives?
   ➤ Singular—Does the position embody a unifying concept?

SWOT Alignment

Once the SWOT variables are identified and prioritized, it is helpful to align the internal strengths and weaknesses with the external opportunities and threats to begin exploring possible strategies.

The template in Figure 5.3 demonstrates the means of aligning the SWOT elements.[2]

Figure 5.3 SWOT Alignment

	Strengths	Weaknesses
Opportunities	Internal strengths matched with external opportunities	Internal weaknesses relative to external opportunities
Threats	Internal strengths matched with external threats	Internal weaknesses relative to external threats

Taking the previous work from the CustoSolution SWOT Analysis, we align the internal and external factors to begin developing possible strategies as shown in Figure 5.4.

Figure 5.4 SWOT Alignment for Strategy

Internal / External	Strengths	Weaknesses
	1. Customer knowledge 2. Established base of contracts 3. Breadth of portfolio	1. Marketing resources 2. Siloed approach to growth 3. R&D investment level 4. Timely resolution of quality issues
Opportunities 1. Product use in outpatient facilities 2. Baby Boomer need 3. Expansion of consulting services	**Possible Strategies** 1. Leverage customer knowledge to drive consulting services in outpatient facilities.	**Possible Strategies** 1. Apply limited marketing resources to the high growth segment of outpatient facilities
Threats 1. Competitor partnerships w/non-traditional players 2. Increasing power of buyers 3. Customers awarding non-exclusive agreements	**Possible Strategies** 1. Build in value-added items (i.e., leadership training) to the established base of contracts to add switching costs that prevent greater use of non-exclusive agreements	**Possible Strategies** 1. Create cross-functional SWAT team to speedily address issues from key customers

Growth Strategies

As kids, we watched Popeye the Sailor Man rip open a can of spinach, wolf it down, and grow big muscles to win the day. If only growing a business was that easy. What specifically are you doing to grow your business? What are the key growth strategies that you're employing to take your business to the next level? A clear understanding of the levers for business growth will dramatically enhance your ability to control your own destiny.

You can assess business growth through both quantitative and qualitative techniques. Gross profit is the most often utilized measurement of growth. Gross profit equals revenues minus the direct costs of goods or services. The value that you create for your customer base is directly correlated with your gross profit.

What metrics does your group employ to measure growth? Are those metrics consistent across the company? A common challenge is differing expectations on what growth looks like. Are you trying to grow revenue, profitability, or market share? If the sales team is measured on revenue growth and the marketing team is evaluated on market share growth, their respective efforts may be working directly against one another.

In the book *Double Digit Growth*, Michael Treacy outlines five growth disciplines that we can configure to build a portfolio of growth strategies for our business.[3]

1. Improve Customer-Base Retention

Gaining new customers and new pieces of business mean nothing if we lose customers and pieces of business at the same rate. In order for growth from new business to substantially improve our standing, we must first ensure that the base of current customers holds firm. There are three guiding principles in maintaining the customer base:

a. Shape the customers' value criteria

The Subway sandwich franchise has successfully taken a significant share of the fast-food dollar by shaping customer's value criteria from speed-of-service and taste to health. By offering customers a healthier alternative to traditional fast food, Subway has shaped the way customers choose their meals and has caused their competitors to offer healthier fare.

b. Increase switching costs

What have you done to make it difficult for customers to leave you for a competitor? GE developed a program called "At the Customer, for the Customer" that has deeply embedded GE in their customers' businesses. Through a portfolio of consulting and training services, GE has packaged their expertise to create greater value for their customers' businesses and in turn, make it more difficult for customers to leave.

c. Narrow customer's alternatives

It stands to reason that the fewer choices your customer has, the greater probability that they will choose to do business with you. That is the rationale behind companies such as Apple and Sony creating their own retail outlets. By designing state-of-the-art stores for consumers to interact with their products and their products only, they are inherently narrowing customers' purchasing alternatives.

2. Take Customers from the Competition

While it can be the most difficult method of growing your business, taking customers from the competition is successfully accomplished every day by thousands of companies. The key to taking business from the competition is to deliver superior value. Delivering superior value starts with consciously selecting which of the three value disciplines to excel in: operational excellence (best total cost), product leadership (best product), or customer intimacy (best total solution). Once the value discipline has been selected, a critical next step is to craft a value proposition that clearly and concisely communicates your value to customers.

3. Staking Claim in the Fastest Growing Market Segment

If stealing customers from the competition is the most difficult way to grow business, positioning yourself in the fastest growing segment of the market may be the easiest. We say easiest because if you're well positioned in the fastest growing segment of the market, your slice of the pie will grow along with the whole. Selecting the right piece of pie is made possible by strategic thinking.

Strategic thinking is the generation of business insights and is propelled by a state of continuous interactivity with the market, customers, competitors, and the organization. Strategic thinking enables you to identify market trends in value criteria, demographics, and innovation before your competitors and leverage them for growth.

4. Moving into Adjacent Markets

For those groups that have mastered the first three growth disciplines, moving into adjacent markets presents a viable opportunity to take growth to the next level. The trick is to determine which adjacent markets have the characteristics that will enable success and which are opportunity quicksand. If the adjacent market differs significantly in cost structure, competitors, customers, or necessary competencies, it may prove difficult to crack. Dell's move from PCs into printers is an example of successfully moving into an adjacent market while Levi's move from jeans to shoes is an example of that alluring quicksand.

5. Jumping into New Lines of Business

A new line of business is one in which your current core competencies are not of great value. A new line of business requires new capabilities and in many circumstances, these capabilities are purchased, as in an acquisition. Richard Branson's appetite for catapulting his Virgin brand into new lines of business ranging from music to cell phones to air travel is legendary. He has started a mind-boggling 350 companies and has demonstrated that venturing into uncharted territory can indeed pay off.

Growth Matrix

Another tool for finding growth in your business is the Growth Matrix. The Growth Matrix concept was introduced by Ram Charan and examines your business on two parameters: needs and customers—both of which are categorized as either "existing" or "new."[4] Figure 5.5 illustrates the Growth Matrix concept and provides an example for each quadrant.

Figure 5.5 Growth Matrix

	Existing	New
New	*Expanding the Pond* Existing Customers With New Needs (Apple & iTunes Music Store)	*New Boat in New Pond* New Customers With New Needs (John Deere Golf & Turf One Source)
Existing	*Expanding share of the Pond* Existing Customers With Existing Needs (Wal-Mart adding groceries)	*Same Boat in New Pond* New Customers With Existing Needs (Avon & teenage market)

Need (vertical axis) — **Customers** (horizontal axis)

The lower left quadrant is *Existing Customers with Existing Needs* or "expanding the share of the pond" as Wal-Mart did when it added groceries. The upper left quadrant is *Existing Customers with New Needs* or "expanding the pond" as Apple Computer did with their iTunes Music Store. The lower right quadrant is *New Customers with Existing Needs* or "same boat in a new pond" as Avon Cosmetics did when they entered the teenage market. And finally, the upper right quadrant is *New Customers with New Needs* or "new boat in a new pond" as John Deere Golf & Turf One Source did in moving into the golf course maintenance business.

Strategy Formula®

As with many higher level disciplines such as medicine, leadership, and law, transforming an abstract concept such as strategy into a tangible one is part science and part art. The scientific aspect comes from the business acumen required to assess and analyze all the moving parts of a dynamic business. The artistic aspect comes from the need to then synthesize all the individual elements into a purposeful system of activity that achieves goals and objectives.

The Strategy Formula has been designed to provide managers with the skeletal framework for strategy, much as the wire frame provides a sculptor with a base for their work of art. The Strategy Formula ensures that the articulation and communication of strategy is sound and consistent across the business unit, functional groups, or organization as a whole. As we noted earlier, key planning terms such as goals, objectives, strategies, and tactics are often used interchangeably and incorrectly. The Strategy Formula helps to eliminate those situations by guiding the process of channeling strategy from mind to paper.

Strategy Formula = WHAT + HOW + WHO + IMPACT

WHAT: The activity or thing being used to accomplish the purpose of the strategy.

HOW: The general means or method of accomplishing the purpose of the strategy.

WHO: The audience that the strategy is designed to reach.

IMPACT: The desired result of creating and implementing
the strategy.

Let's review two examples of the Strategy Formula in action
in the medical device arena:

Strategy Example 1:
Objectively determine which customers to acquire and which
customers not to acquire by developing and implementing a
Customer Selection Criteria System to enable the sales force
to more effectively allocate their resources and enhance the
division's profitability.

Strategy Formula Breakdown:
WHAT: Objectively determine which customers to acquire
and which customers not to acquire...
HOW: ...by developing and implementing a Customer
Selection Criteria System
WHO: ...sales force...
IMPACT: ...to more effectively allocate their resources and
enhance the division's profitability.

Strategy Example 2:
Create a for-fee business consulting service to complement
product offerings that provides hospital executive teams with
process systems expertise relative to strategy formulation and
execution in order to deepen relationships and better understand customer's strategic perspectives.

Strategy Formula Breakdown:
WHAT: Create a for-fee business consulting service...
HOW: ...by providing process systems expertise relative to
strategy formulation and execution...
WHO: ....hospital executive teams...
IMPACT: ...to deepen relationships and better understand
customer's strategic perspectives.

StrategyPrint

Until now, one of the greatest challenges in strategic planning has been linking the strategic plan with day-to-day activities. Typically, lengthy strategic plans are housed in bulky three-ring binders collecting dust on the shelf until their annual renewal. The solution to this age-old dilemma is to morph the traditional narrative strategic plan into a concise but thorough business blueprint, or StrategyPrint, that managers can use every day to drive their activities.

The StrategyPrint is a powerful two-page blueprint that serves as a real-time strategic action plan for your business. The StrategyPrint solves the challenge of linking strategy development with strategy execution by providing a concise yet thorough two-page document that is infinitely more functional to use on a daily basis than the traditional strategic plan.

Page one of the StrategyPrint (Figure 5.6) captures the key insights for the business and places them in the four categories of market, customers, competition, and the company. The intelligence and insights are generated during the discovery and strategic thinking phases of the process.

Page two of the StrategyPrint (Figure 5.7) transforms the insights into the strategic action plan, including the overarching strategy, critical success factors, goals, objectives, strategies, and tactics. The result is a common planning framework that can be used throughout your group to ensure that everyone is following a unified strategic direction.

The example provided for CustoSolution contains the areas that best meet their business planning needs (i.e., Managed Care Overview, Critical Success Factors, etc.). The Strate-

Figure 5.6 StrategyPrint Page 1

CUSTOSOLUTION STRATEGYPRINT®

MARKET

STATE
- Market growth is 6%
- No new entrants

TRENDS
- Baby Boomers retiring and impact on Medicare
- Preference for smaller, cross-platform devices
- Heightened consumer knowledge on treatments

MANAGED CARE OVERVIEW
- Group Purchasing Organization's increase in buying power
- Move to non-exclusive contracts

COMPANY

STRENGTHS
- Customer knowledge due to consulting services
- Established base of contracts
- Breadth of product portfolio

WEAKNESSES
- Non-competitive marketing resources (outspent 3:1)
- Siloed approach to growth
- R&D investment level (outspent 5:1)
- Timely resolution of customer quality issues (60 days)

OPPORTUNITIES
- Outpatient facilities product use (25% of mkt)
- Baby boomer segment (2/3 of patients)
- Expansion of consulting services (75% of current product customers not using)

THREATS
- Competitor partnerships with non-traditional players
- Increasing power of buyers
- Customers awarding non-exclusive agreements (35%)

CUSTOMERS

TOP 10 ACCOUNTS	PRODUCT CHOICE	YTD REVENUE
1. Kaiser	TechnoStar	$ 22,000
2. Northwestern	TechnoStar	$ 12,000
3. Mayo Clinic	CustoSolution	$ 450,000
4. US Gov't.	CostAlert	$ 6,000
5. UCLA	CustoSolution	$ 397,500
6. U of Arizona	TechnoStar	$ 44,000
7. Sloan-Kettering	TechnoStar	$ 0
8. U of Chicago	CustoSolution	$ 285,000
9. U of Texas	CostAlert	$ 8,400
10. Advocate	CustoSolution	$ 77,000

COMPETITORS

	TechnoStar	CostAlert
MARKET SHARE	37.3%	16.7%
STRENGTHS	- R&D investment - Marketing - Technology platform	- Operational effectiveness
WEAKNESSES	- Breadth of product line	- Inferior technology - R&D resources - Marketing platform
CORE MESSAGE	"Cutting-edge technology"	"Cost-effective technology"
PRICE POSITION	High	Low
COMPETITIVE ACTIVITIES	- Customer CEO Roundtable Symposiums - Thought-Leader Training	- Price-cutting in high-volume accounts

Figure 5.7 StrategyPrint Page 2
CUSTOSOLUTION STRATEGYPRINT®

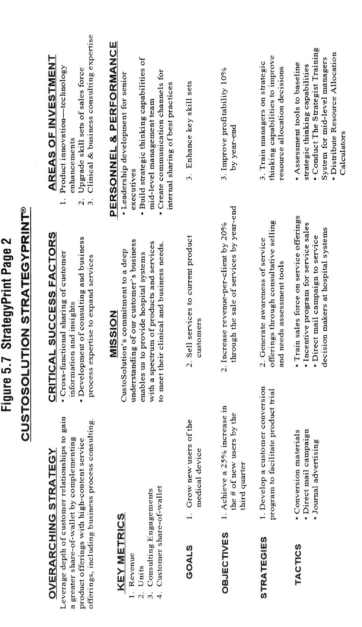

OVERARCHING STRATEGY

Leverage depth of customer relationships to gain a greater share-of-wallet by complementing product offerings with high-content service offerings, including business process consulting.

KEY METRICS

1. Revenue
2. Units
3. Consulting Engagements
4. Customer share-of-wallet

GOALS

1. Grow new users of the medical device

OBJECTIVES

1. Achieve a 25% increase in the # of new users by the third quarter

STRATEGIES

1. Develop a customer conversion program to facilitate product trial

TACTICS

- Conversion materials
- Direct mail campaign
- Journal advertising

CRITICAL SUCCESS FACTORS

- Cross-functional sharing of customer information and insights
- Development of consulting and business process expertise to expand services

MISSION

CustoSolution's commitment to a deep understanding of our customer's business enables us to provide hospital systems with a spectrum of products and services to meet their clinical and business needs.

2. Sell services to current product customers

2. Increase revenue-per-client by 20% through the sale of services by year-end

2. Generate awareness of service offerings through consultative selling and needs assessment tools

- Train sales force on service offerings
- Incentive program for service sales
- Direct mail campaign to service decision makers at hospital systems

AREAS OF INVESTMENT

1. Product innovation—technology enhancements
2. Upgrade skill sets of sales force
3. Clinical & business consulting expertise

PERSONNEL & PERFORMANCE

- Leadership development for senior executives
- Build strategic thinking capabilities of mid-level management team
- Create communication channels for internal sharing of best practices

3. Enhance key skill sets

3. Improve profitability 10% by year-end

3. Train managers on strategic thinking capabilities to improve resource allocation decisions

- Assessment tools to baseline strategic thinking capabilities
- Conduct The Strategist Training System for mid-level managers
- Distribute Resource Allocation Calculators

gyPrint is customized for each individual company, using the language that the group is accustomed to in order to make it as relevant and easy-to-use as possible. The StrategyPrint embodies the premise "brevity demonstrates mastery." In a time when we are expected to move at warp speed and communicate instantaneously, the StrategyPrint enables you to quickly and comprehensively convey the key aspects of your business to colleagues, the Board of Directors, employees, or venture capitalists. It also leads to greater accountability because the strategies, tactics and owners are clearly apparent on the two-page framework instead of being buried in a thick document.

Real-Time Strategy

The result of using the StrategyPrint is real-time strategy. Because the StrategyPrint is in a concise, two-page format, it is used and updated on a daily basis. The result of having a tool that can be updated in real time to reflect new insights is simply:

Better—Strategy—Faster

Shaping strategy in a continuous manner produces a virtuous cascade that includes revenue, profitability, productivity, and cost savings. Strategy's virtuous cascade is depicted in Figure 5.8.

The StrategyPrint houses the strategic filters (i.e., purpose, business design, strategy, etc.) that act as criteria for resource allocation decisions. The strategic filters ensure that our resources are used as effectively and efficiently as possible, which means more capital, talent, and time (resources) invested in the right activities and less in the wrong activities. This

Figure 5.8 Strategy's Virtuous Cascade

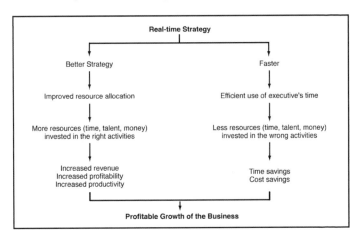

leads to increased revenue, profitability, productivity, capital savings, and time savings—ultimately, the profitable growth of the business.

DIFFERENCE MAKERS

- Strategic planning takes the insights generated from the discovery and strategic thinking phases and channels them into an action plan to achieve goals and objectives.

- Business Model Analysis—A concise method of determining the context, who, what, how, and strategy shield that comprise the building blocks of a business.

- Purpose—Mission, vision, and values.

- Value Discipline—The decision to focus on one of the following three disciplines: 1) operational excellence, 2) product leadership, or 3) customer intimacy.

- Value Proposition—A clearly articulated statement of the value you deliver to customers.

- Position—The place you want your offering to own in the customer's mind.

- SWOT Alignment—A matrix designed to combine the internal capabilities (strengths and weaknesses) with the external possibilities (opportunities and threats) to begin thinking about strategies.

- Growth Disciplines—Thoughtful selection of the following five growth strategies to create a portfolio of initiatives to grow the business.
  1. Improve Customer-Base Retention
  2. Take Customers from the Competition
  3. Staking Claim in the Fastest Growing Market Segment
  4. Moving into Adjacent Markets
  5. Jumping into New Lines of Business

Continued on next page

- Growth Matrix—Tool used for examining your business on two parameters: Needs and Customers—both of which are categorized as either existing or new.

- The Strategy Formula has been designed to provide managers with the skeletal framework for strategy and ensures that the articulation and communication of strategy is sound and consistent across the business unit, functional groups, or organization as a whole.

- Strategy Formula = WHAT + HOW + WHO + IMPACT

  WHAT: The activity or thing being used to accomplish the purpose of the strategy.
  HOW: The general means or method of accomplishing the purpose of the strategy.
  WHO: The audience that the strategy is designed to reach.
  IMPACT: The desired result of creating and implementing the strategy.

- The StrategyPrint is a powerful two-page blueprint that serves as a real-time strategic action plan or map for your business. The StrategyPrint solves the challenge of linking strategy development with strategy execution by providing a concise and thorough two-page document that is infinitely more functional to use on a daily basis than the traditional strategic plan.

- Page one of the StrategyPrint captures the key insights for the business regarding the market, customers, competition, and the organization.

- Page two of the StrategyPrint transforms the insights into the strategic action plan, including the overarching strategy, business drivers, goals, objectives, strategies, and tactics.

- The StrategyPrint fosters real-time strategy because its concise two-page format allows it to be easily updated on a daily basis.

CHAPTER 6

Strategy Rollout

"Sculpting the Masterpiece"

*There are risks and costs to a program of action.
But they are far less than the long-range risks
and costs of comfortable inaction.*

– John F. Kennedy
Former President of the United States

Once the framework has been developed, the artist sculpts the figure, adding and taking away material as necessary. In the same way, the strategy rollout phase transforms the strategic plan into the actions that move the business forward. Just as a plumbing system moves water to all of the appropriate locations within your home, the implementation plan provides the piping for moving strategic direction throughout your organization. Not having a strong pipeline to all of the functional groups in the organization may cause information leaks that can derail your efforts.

The strategy rollout phase ensures that the key elements of the strategic plan are clearly communicated throughout the organization and that an implementation plan is in place. The first step is to create an overarching implementation plan that provides the direction and detail of how the strategic plan will be executed. Following is a checklist of the key areas to address in designing a solid implementation plan:

❑ **Purpose**—What purposes is the plan designed to achieve? Are they clearly articulated in the form of vision, goals, and objectives?

❑ **Resources**—What are the resources (capital, talent, and time) that will be allocated to achieve the plan's purposes?

❑ **Accountability**—Which individuals and functional groups are assigned responsibility for achieving each of the goals?

❑ **Time Frame**—What are the time parameters associated with the elements of the plan?

❑ **Budget**—How much will each item identified in the plan cost to implement?

❑ **Alignment**—Are all of the functional groups (marketing, sales, project management, IT, etc.) aligned to achieve the same goals or will groups be pulling in different directions?

❑ **Metrics**—Are clear, consistent, and realistic metrics in place to monitor progress?

❑ **Project Template**—Is a singular project template in place to ensure that all projects consuming resources are meeting the agreed upon strategic criteria?

❏ **Communication Tools**—Have the appropriate communication vehicles been identified to convey the key information of the strategic plan to all employees?

Resource Allocation Calculator

As the essence of strategy involves resource allocation, it is imperative to have sufficient resources to implement the designated strategies. A useful tool for gauging the sufficiency of resources to implement a strategy is the Resource Allocation (RA) Calculator.

Using the RA Calculator, the three areas of resources (capital, talent, and time) are assessed on the required level versus the actual level. If the actual level of resources is greater than or equal to the required level of resources for an area, the area is green-lighted. If the actual level of resources is less than the required level of resources, the area is red-lighted to indicate a potential danger to successful execution of the strategy. If strategies with less than the required level of resources are still pursued, they are marked moving forward with a yellow light to indicate the decision to proceed with less than adequate resources.

Example:

Goal: Increase number of new users for TechnoStar's medical device.

Objective: Achieve a 75% penetration rate for high and medium users of such devices for the East region by year end.

Strategy: Leverage national opinion leaders to create renewed interest among surgeons at academic and community hospitals in reassessing treatment protocols that don't currently prioritize TechnoStar's device.

Figure 6.0 RA Calculator

Resources	Required	Actual	Gap	Status
Capital	$75k	$80k	None	Green
Talent	3 Sales Reps 1 Sales Manager 1 National Account Mgr	2 Sales Reps 1 Sales Manager 1 National Account Mgr	1 Sales Rep	Red
Time	70 hours	70 hours	None	Green

From these calculations, we can make the following deductions:

- Capital requirements are met with a surplus, so it is green-lighted.

- Talent requirements are not met because one additional sales rep is required, so it is red-lighted until further review.

- Time requirements are met, so it is green-lighted.

The RA Calculator removes the guess work from strategy execution by breaking resources down into their individual components and providing clarity around their chances for success. It also gives ammunition to those managers seeking more resources by concisely outlining a mini-business case for their request.

Strategy Rollout

Once the overarching implementation plan has been developed and resource levels assessed, there are five steps to a smooth strategy rollout as depicted in Figure 6.1:

Figure 6.1 Strategy Rollout

1. Develop a Communication Plan

After the strategic plan has been crafted, the communications plan is created to facilitate the sharing of the strategic plan elements with all relevant stakeholders. Kevin Rollins, CEO of Dell, highlights an important aspect of the communications effort: "You have to modify messages by constituency. Which elements of the overall strategy do you want to discuss with each constituent? The communication function breaks strategy into pieces and sells the right pieces to the right audience."[1]

A Strategic Communications Matrix (Figure 6.2) can be a helpful outline for the communications plan because it ensures that the right messages are being channeled to the right audiences with the right vehicles.

119

Figure 6.2 Strategic Communications Matrix

Communication Goals	Constituencies	Vehicles
Internal Alignment on Strategy	- Employees	- StrategyPrint - Training Programs: Workbooks, CD-ROMs - Newsletters - Town Hall Meetings - Presentations - Posters/Desk Signage
External Guide on Strategic Direction	- Investors - Customers - Media	- Conference Calls - Press Releases - Executive Interviews
Commitment to Purpose (Mission, Vision, Values)	- Employees - Communities - Investors - Media	- Advertising - Event Sponsorship - Philanthropy - Wallet cards - Internal Signage
Using Strategy to Drive Growth (Revenue, Profitability, Market Share, etc.)	- Customers by Segments & Targets	- Sales materials - Advertising - Trade Shows - Symposia

Prior to the development of the communication vehicles, use the communication goals and the range of audiences along with their perspectives for the most appropriate selection of tools. While universal strategic themes are important to driving consistency across the communication efforts, tailoring the meaning or "So what?" of the strategic plan for the individual constituencies is a crucial task.

2. Communicate the Strategic Plan

There are five keys to successfully communicating the strategic plan to members of the organization:

1. **Simplicity**— set expectations with a universally understood language.

2. **Clarity**—identify clear objectives with a concise message.

3. **Repetition**—develop a feedback loop to continue communicating the messages after the initial campaign. As George Bernard Shaw said, "The greatest problem with communication is the illusion that it has been accomplished."

4. **Interaction**—include forums for open, honest, and two-way communication with employees to capture feedback for modifying the message.

5. **Multiple vehicles**—utilize a number of different mediums to share the plan's information.

3. Collect and Review Feedback

Formal and informal methods for collecting and reviewing feedback on the strategic plan should be included in the process to determine the breadth and depth of the plan's understanding by employees. Formal methods include surveys, town hall meetings, and individual interviews. Informal methods include cafeteria conversations, Q&A sessions at the functional or business unit level, and email correspondence. While the members of the strategy development team will have an intricate understanding of the strategic plan at this point, it should not be taken for granted that the other employees will have that same level of understanding.

4. Incorporate Into Daily Activities

The strategy rollout uses the primary elements of the strategic plan to drive employees' daily activities. When strategy is used to drive daily activities, it can then be seamlessly woven into an employee's action plan, accountabilities, and compensation program.

Strategy is most effectively incorporated into employees' daily activities using the tools that they consult on a regular basis to guide their work. The StrategyPrint serves in this capacity because it is designed to be used by employees at all levels and in the various functional groups, ensuring that their efforts are aligned with the overarching goals and strategies of the organization.

5. Monitor Progress

The interactive and dynamic nature of business requires the ability to think strategically on a daily basis. In that spirit, we must continually monitor not only the validity and relevance of the strategy itself, but also the implementation and communication of that strategy.

Obviously, the metrics you choose will provide the key gauge as to whether the organization is aligned and working toward the strategic direction outlined. Organizations can become awash in metrics and easily lose sight of their goals and strategies. Select metrics discriminately, using only the handful that will truly measure the progress you are trying to achieve. Be sure to measure not only the strategy's effectiveness, but also the effectiveness of the *communication* of the strategy internally with employees and externally with the appropriate stakeholders.

- The strategy rollout phase ensures that the key elements of the strategic plan are clearly communicated throughout the organization and that an implementation plan is in place.

- A checklist of the key areas to address in designing a solid implementation and communication plan includes:

  - Purpose—What purposes is the plan designed to achieve and are they clearly articulated in the form of vision, goals, and objectives?

  - Resources—What are the resources (capital, talent, and time) that will be required to achieve the plan's purposes?

  - Accountability—Which individuals and functional groups are assigned responsibility for achieving each of the goals?

  - Time Frame—What are the time parameters associated with the elements of the plan?

  - Budget—How much will each item identified in the plan cost to implement?

  - Alignment—Are all of the functional groups (marketing, sales, project management, IT, etc.) aligned to achieve the same goals or will groups be pulling in different directions?

  - Metrics—Are clear, consistent, and realistic metrics in place to monitor progress?

Continued on next page

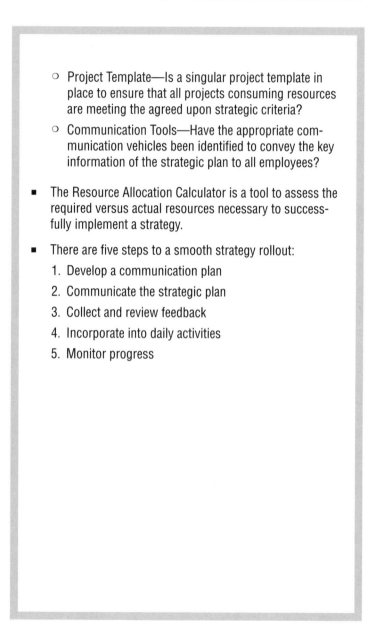

○ Project Template—Is a singular project template in place to ensure that all projects consuming resources are meeting the agreed upon strategic criteria?

○ Communication Tools—Have the appropriate communication vehicles been identified to convey the key information of the strategic plan to all employees?

- The Resource Allocation Calculator is a tool to assess the required versus actual resources necessary to successfully implement a strategy.

- There are five steps to a smooth strategy rollout:
  1. Develop a communication plan
  2. Communicate the strategic plan
  3. Collect and review feedback
  4. Incorporate into daily activities
  5. Monitor progress

CHAPTER 7

Strategy Tune-up

"Polishing the Form"

Few things are impossible to diligence and skill.
Great works are performed not by strength,
but perseverance.

– Samuel Johnson
English Writer

Once the sculptor finishes her work, she must ensure that adjustments, such as proper lighting, and maintenance activities, including cleaning and polishing, are performed on a regular basis to keep the sculpture looking its best. Similarly, the strategy tune-up phase serves to keep the strategy evergreen.

We use the term "tune-up" to signify the importance of reviewing strategy and the assumptions at its foundation on a regularly scheduled basis. Most people don't drive their car for an entire year without attending to it on a periodic basis—getting oil changes, having tires rotated, fluids refilled, etc. Yet countless organizations, business units, and brand teams will go a full year before reviewing their strategy. On the whole, they take better preventative care of their automobiles than their organizations.

The strategy tune-up phase is a periodic formal review of the strategy by the strategy development team. Consisting of a half to one day session on a quarterly basis, the team reviews the key areas of the business (market, customers, competitors, and organization) to identify significant changes and make adjustments in strategy and tactics. The strategy tune-up prevents the organization from missing market trend shifts, changes in customer demand, and other events that can make current resource allocations obsolete.

Prior to the strategy tune-up session, the strategy development team leader should provide team members with an insight collection tool such as the Strategy Survey. This will give team members a mechanism to refocus their thinking, challenge assumptions, and objectively review the elements of the strategic plan prior to the meeting. The pre-session preparation also maximizes the group's meeting time by giving members the opportunity to think through the finer points of the business.

The strategy tune-up session is facilitated by the team leader and follows an abbreviated version of the process outlined in the strategic thinking phase. The strategy tune-up sessions are critical to the health of the business and should have a priority level similar to that of a Board of Director's meeting. The dates of the sessions should be planned out well in advance (one year if possible) and not moved or missed.

The strategy tune-up's methodical review of the market, customers, competitors, and the organization is important because it ensures that all the relevant areas of the business are examined. Otherwise, it is too easy to spend the entire session on an urgent but tangential and low-priority issue that gathers momentum and consumes all of the allotted time. Background information and data should be distributed to team members prior to the strategy tune-up to maximize the productivity of the face-to-face meeting time. Again, it is one of the crucial responsibilities of the strategy development team leader to create an assertive agenda, select appropriate models, and skillfully move the discussion forward.

Once the abbreviated group strategic thinking process is completed, the team turns its attention to the StrategyPrint and any other strategic planning tools. The team assesses the goals, objectives, strategies, tactics, and metrics to determine if and where any resource allocation changes are warranted. These modifications of resource allocation can also benefit from the creation of a Strategic Reserve.

Strategic Reserve

The concept of the Strategic Reserve is based on the Rapid Deployment Force (RDF). The Rapid Deployment Force consists of a select number of individuals and resources from existing American military forces.[1] The RDF was designed to embody the following characteristics:

- Intentionally held back and not committed to one particular place
- Highly mobile
- Existed in a high state of readiness
- Reported to the highest strategic decision-making levels
- Small enough to be mobile but large enough to make an impact

A useful application of the RDF for businesses is the Strategic Reserve.[2] The goal of a strategic reserve is to add resources, talent, and energy where they will have the greatest impact. Too often, the line items of a budget are etched in stone at the beginning of the fiscal year, providing for little if any adaptation to changing business conditions as the year progresses. Creating a strategic reserve enables you to further bolster the strategies and tactics that are proving successful by channeling the strategic reserve resources into those activities to maximize their effectiveness. The strategic reserve concept can be successfully utilized in all areas of the business, from R&D through marketing.

Deliberately maintaining resources (capital, time from current personnel, new personnel) in a line item called "strategic reserve" eliminates the difficult task of pulling resources from other groups or areas in midstream. It also avoids the political backwaters by not forcing the withdrawal of resources from any specific person or functional group. The Strategic Reserve is tapped into when you believe that an emerging opportunity or a current success would add exponentially more value to the business if supplied with additional resources. These resources, which may include money, equipment, personnel, or personnel's time allocation, are then deployed to the opportunity or successful strategy to "add fuel to the fire."

The Strategic Reserve is simply used where it can provide the "biggest-bang-for-the-buck." Avoid the temptation of using the Strategic Reserve to shore up a weak spot in the business. A weak spot is usually a weak spot for a reason. More times than not, putting additional resources into a weak area is like giving additional fuel to a sinking ship.

Strategy Renewal

The team should leave the strategy tune-up session with a revised StrategyPrint that reflects the key changes to the business. The team members are then responsible for sharing the notable changes with their colleagues from the various functional units.

Some will ask if strategy should change at all during the strategy tune-up phase because of strategy's "long-term" nature. This mindset has perpetuated one of the great myths in business—"strategy is long-term and tactics are short-term." The current use of "strategic" and "tactical" stems from World War II. "Strategic" became associated with the completely incidental quality of long-range aircraft and missiles, while "tactical" referred to shorter-range aircraft and missiles.[3]

The duration of a strategy then is not based on a set period of one, three, or five years. Strategy is based on the length of time it takes for the resources allocated to yield the desired return on their investment. Therefore, a strategy could last seven months or seven years, depending on the rate of return on the resources invested and the changing dynamics of the market. The difference between strategy and tactics is not length of time, but rather how generally (strategy) or how specifically (tactics) they achieve your goals and objectives.

DIFFERENCE MAKERS

- The strategy tune-up is a periodic formal review of the strategy by the strategy development team. Consisting of a half to one day session on a quarterly basis, the team reviews the key areas of the business (market, customers, competitors, and organization) to identify significant changes and make adjustments in strategy and tactics.

- Once the abbreviated group strategic thinking process is completed, the team turns its attention to the StrategyPrint and any other strategic plan tools. The team assesses the goals, objectives, strategies, tactics and metrics to determine if and where any resource allocation variations are warranted.

- The Rapid Deployment Force concept was designed to embody the following characteristics:
  - Intentionally held back and not committed to one particular place
  - Highly mobile
  - Existed in a high state of readiness
  - Reported to the highest strategic decision-making levels
  - Small enough to be mobile but large enough to make an impact

- A Strategic Reserve is based on the Rapid Deployment Force concept. The goal of a strategic reserve is to add resources, talent, and energy where they will have the greatest impact.

- The duration of a strategy is not based on a set period of one, three, or five years. Strategy is based on the length of time it takes for the resources allocated to yield the desired return on their investment.

- The difference between strategy and tactics is not length of time but rather how generally (strategy) or how specifically (tactics) they achieve the goals and objectives.

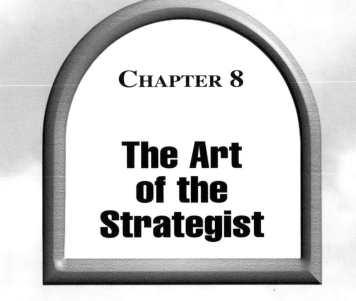

CHAPTER 8

The Art of the Strategist

There's a fine line between fishing and just standing on the shore like an idiot.

– Steven Wright
Comedian

Look around your organization—are people fishing or simply standing on the shore?

Much of what gets passed off as "strategy" in today's business arena is nothing more than shadows of business insight wrapped in vanilla packages of operational tactics. The abstract nature of strategy has permitted this outgrowth of misuse and strangled its true meaning like so many weeds in a garden. "Sculpting air," or shaping strategy, is indeed a challenging task and one that never is fully complete. Nonetheless, as executives it is our responsibility to champion the effort of engaging a strong strategy development process and keeping it evergreen. The fact that you have invested the time to reach this point in the book demonstrates a rare discipline to strategy expertise that few of your peers possess.

Research has shown that sound strategy development and execution are absolute requirements for long-term financial success—no exceptions. Yet, many companies spend less than 10% of their time on strategic issues and allow the urgent—not the important—to dominate their business. This is akin to jumping out of an airplane with no parachute and yelling, "Hey, where's my lucky nickel?"

A solid strategy development process is simple, concise, and effective. It provides direction without telling you how to build the compass. It generates insights into the business without miring you in the muck of extraneous elements. And it stimulates the profitable growth of your business without the rambling, off-course meetings that foster meaningless projects that suck the life out of good people.

The best-of-breed strategy development process produces the following benefits:

1. Transparency of key business insights across the different functional units.

2. Strategic filters that improve decision making and resource allocation.

3. List of critical issues to frame the management team's work.

4. Strategic action plan that guides and profitably grows the business.

5. Optimal positioning of the company, product, or service for competitive advantage.

6. Focus and unity of effort across the organization on the key success factors.

Just as the sculptor follows a methodical process to create something from nothing, so too do we follow a process to shape strategy:

I.   Discovery—"Choosing the Tools"
II. Strategic Thinking—"Playing in Space"
III. Strategic Planning—"Building the Framework"
IV. Strategy Rollout—"Sculpting the Masterpiece"
V.   Strategy Tune-up—"Polishing the Form"

StrategySphere System®

 → → → → Strategy Tune-up (1 day/Qtr.)

Discovery (1-4 weeks)	Strategic Thinking (2-3 days)	Strategic Planning (1-2 days)	Strategy Rollout (2-4 weeks)	Strategy Tune-up (1 day/Qtr.)
• Designation of strategy development team	• **Market** Structure State & Trends PEST Analysis Scenario Projection	• **Company** Mission, Vision, Values Value Discipline Position Value Proposition SWOT Alignment Growth Strategies Strategic Message	• Development of Implementation & Communication Plan	• StrategyPrint review & modification
• Briefing session (1/2 day)	• **Customers** Segment Matrix 80/20 Analysis Decision Tree Value Drivers Satisfaction Gauge Service Map	• **StrategyPrint** Summary of Insights Goals Objectives Strategies Tactics Metrics	• Strategy Rollout 1. Development of communication plan 2. Communications to group 3. Collect & review feedback 4. Incorporate into daily activities 5. Monitor progress	
• Assignment of pre-work Strategy Survey Market Research Intelligence Compilation Market Customers Competitors Company	• **Competitors** Offerings Strengths & Weaknesses Strategic Profile Competitor Attributes Competitive Advantage Position			
• Interviews	• **Company** SWOT Analysis Opportunity & Threat Matrices Business Model Analysis Activity System Map			

133

Somewhere between the mountains of complex theory and the mole hills of ignorant bliss lies the essence of strategy. Although we can't see it or touch it, we know strategy in its simplest form is composed of the three A's of acumen, allocation, and action. This knowledge along with a steady process for crafting, shaping, and honing strategy provides all the tools necessary to create a business masterpiece.

Only one question remains: Will you or your competition be holding the chisel?

Notes

Chapter 1

1. William Joyce, Nitin Nohria, and Bruce Roberson, *What (Really) Works* (New York: HarperCollins Publishers, 2003).
2. Joan Lublin and Mark Maremont, "Taking Tyco by the Tail," *Wall Street Journal*, August 6, 2003.
3. Michael Mankins, "Stop Wasting Valuable Time," *Harvard Business Review*, September 2004.
4. Patricia Sellers and Julie Schlosser, "It's His Home Depot Now," *Fortune Magazine*, September 20, 2004.
5. Sun Tzu, edited by James Clavell, *The Art of War* (New York: Delacorte Press, 1983).
6. Michael Porter, "What is Strategy?" *Harvard Business Review*, November – December 1996.
7. Porter, "What is Strategy?" *Harvard Business Review*, November - December 1996.
8. Bruce Henderson, "The Origin of Strategy," *Harvard Business Review*, November - December 1989.
9. Jeffrey Immelt, "Letter to Stakeholders," *GE 2003 Annual Report*, February 13, 2004.
10. Erick Schonfeld, "How to Manage Growth," *Business 2.0*, December 2004.
11. Porter, "What is Strategy?" *Harvard Business Review*, November - December 1996.

Chapter 2

1. Andrew Campbell, "Discovering Significant and Viable New Businesses: Have Faith in Strategic Planning Basics," *Strategy and Leadership*, Vol. 33 No. 1, 2005.
2. Tim Brown, "Strategy by Design," *Fast Company*, June 2005.

Chapter 4

1. Art Kleiner, "GE's Next Workout," *Strategy + Business*, Issue 33.
2. Ibid., 27.
3. Ibid., 30.
4. Ibid.

5. Jeffrey Immelt, "Letter to Stakeholders," *GE 2003 Annual Report*, February 13, 2004.
6. Milind Lele, *Creating Strategic Leverage* (New York: John Wiley & Sons, 1992).
7. Michael Porter, *Competitive Strategy* (New York: The Free Press, 1980).
8. H. James Harrington, *Business Process Improvement* (New York: Mc-Graw-Hill, 1991).
9. Ibid.
10. W. Chan Kim and Renée Mauborgne, "Charting Your Company's Future," *Harvard Business Review*, June 2002.
11. Porter, "What is Strategy?" *Harvard Business Review*, November - December 1996.
12. Kevin Coyne, "Sustainable Competitive Advantage," *The McKinsey Quarterly*, November 1984.
13. Bruce Chew, "The Geometry of Competition," The Monitor Group, 2000.
14. Peter Drucker, "Why Management Consultants," *Perspectives,* The Boston Consulting Group, 1981.
15. Terry Richey, *The Marketer's Visual Tool Kit* (New York: AMACOM, 1994).

Chapter 5

1. Michael Treacy and Fred Wiersema, *The Discipline of Market Leaders* (New York: Perseus Books, 1995).
2. H. Weihrich, "The TOWS Matrix—A Tool for Situational Analysis," *Long Range Planning*, 1982.
3. Michael Treacy, *Double-Digit Growth* (New York: Portfolio, 2003).
4. Ram Charan, *Profitable Growth is Everyone's Business* (New York: Crown Business, 2004).

Chapter 6

1. Paul Argenti, et al, "The Strategic Communication Imperative," *MIT Sloan Management Review*, Spring 2005.

Chapter 7

1. Evan Dudik, *Strategic Renaissance* (New York: AMACOM, 2000).
2. Ibid.
3. Edward Luttwak, *Strategy: The Logic of War and Peace* (Cambridge, MA: The Belknap Press of Harvard University Press, 2001).

Index

About the Author

Rich Horwath is the founder and president of Sculptura Consulting, Inc., a strategy consulting and training firm dedicated to helping companies think strategically to guide and grow their business. He is a former Chief Strategy Officer and works with clients ranging from *Fortune* 100 companies to emerging growth companies located in the U.S., Canada and Europe. He is the author of *Storm Rider: Becoming a Strategic Thinker* and is frequently asked to speak to executive management teams on a range of strategy-related topics including strategic thinking, competitive advantage and growth strategies.

Mr. Horwath's laser-like focus on strategy expertise has resulted in the development of proprietary tools to help managers think strategically about their business. To facilitate strategy development, he designed a simple five-step process called the StrategySphere System®. To assist managers in linking their strategic plans with daily activities, he created the StrategyPrint®—a two-page business blueprint that serves as a concise, real-time strategic action plan—ensuring that all resources and activities are aligned with the overall strategy. And to help managers at all levels become more effective strategists, Mr. Horwath designed the Strategist Training System® which consists of nine different programs delivered in an interactive workshop format.

He earned an MBA with Distinction from the Kellstadt Graduate School of Business at DePaul University and has received Executive Education Program Certificates in Strategy from the University of Chicago Graduate School of Business and the Amos Tuck School of Business Administration at Dartmouth College. He resides in Barrington Hills, Illinois.

Develop better strategy faster

➤ Order additional copies of *Sculpting Air: The Executive's Guide to Shaping Strategy*.

➤ Order your free copy of the StrategySphere System® CD-ROM demo which contains interactive strategic thinking models and the StrategyPrint®—the two-page, real-time strategic plan.

➤ Contact Rich to learn more about his strategy development services.

Outthink the competition

The Strategist Training System® is designed to enhance your manager's strategic thinking capabilities, leading to more effective resource allocation and increased revenue, profitability and productivity.

Participant Level	Programs
Level I: Strategist - Marketing Manager - Product Manager - Brand Manager - Sales Manager	1. The Fundamentals of Business Planning 2. Strategy Made Simple 3. Creating the Strategic Plan
Level II: Advanced Strategist - Associate Director - Director - Vice President	1. Advanced Business Planning 2. Strategic Decision Making 3. Designing Growth Strategies
Level III: Master Strategist - Senior/Executive Vice President - General Manager - President - C-Suite Executives	1. Strategic Leadership: Creating the Big Picture 2. The Executive Program on Shaping Strategy 3. Systems Thinking: A Holistic View of the Business

➤ Select one program or a series of programs for your management team.

➤ Order copies of the book *Storm Rider: Becoming a Strategic Thinker*.

Contact Rich Horwath today at (847) 756-4707
Email rich@sculpturaconsulting.com or visit
www.sculpturaconsulting.com